Cowboy Cocktails

Boot Scootin' Beverages
and Tasty Vittles
from the Wild West

Cowboy Cocktails

Grady Spears & Brigit L. Binns

Food and drink photography
by Rhonda Hole

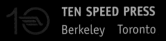

TEN SPEED PRESS
Berkeley   Toronto

Ten Speed Press
PO Box 7123
Berkeley, California 94707
www.tenspeed.com

Distributed in Australia by Simon and Schuster Australia, in Canada by Ten Speed Press Canada, in New Zealand by Southern Publishers Group, in South Africa by Real Books, in Southeast Asia by Berkeley Books, and in the United Kingdom and Europe by Airlift Books.

Cover and text design by Toni Tajima based on a design by Catherine Jacobes
Food styling by Brooke Leonard
Props provided by Prairie Rose, Fort Worth, Texas (817-332-4369) and Leigh Boyd, Fort Worth, Texas (817-738-3705)

Library of Congress Cataloging-in-Publication Data
Spears, Grady.
  Cowboy cocktails: boot scootin' beverages and tasty vittles from the wild west / Grady Spears and Brigit Binns.
    p. cm.
  Includes index.
  ISBN 1-58008-077-4 (pbk.)
  1. Cocktails. 2. Cookery, American—Western style. I. Binns, Brigit Legere. II. Title.
TX951.S667 2000
641.8'74—dc21   99-051837

First printing, 2000
Printed in Hong Kong

1 2 3 4 5 6 7 8 9 10 — 03 02 01 00

Contents

Introduction

IN THE SIMPLEST WHITTLING-DOWN OF LANGUAGE, a cowboy was just a guy who messed around with cows. But in the fantastic, romantic lore of the Wild West, he was infinitely more.

A cowboy was brave and tough and often a bit ornery. He could rassle a 1,000-pound bull to the ground, brand him with a hot iron, and eat his cojones for breakfast. Men and cows feared him, dogs adored him, women waited for him, and children everywhere longed to walk in his boots. Cowboys came to be synonymous with what was special about America. To many generations of non-Americans and hopeful immigrants in the first half of the twentieth century, everyone who lived in the American West was a cowboy. The open range, the call of the wild, and the guitar on his back were symbols of a true cowboy lifestyle that many aspired—lifestyle that truly only existed for the last two or three decades of the nineteenth century. After that, the new barbed-wire fences hemmed him in, laws limited his carousing, and later, movies made him into a dandy. But for much of the twentieth century, urban and suburban cowboys from Texas to New York to Beijing have been aspiring to the rugged identity of this enduring and compelling icon of manhood. There is little doubt that the romance and individuality of the cowboy will continue to motivate imitators well into the twenty-first century.

After the Civil War ended, the wounded but recovering country was ready to rebuild and expand, and the only place to expand was west. But the wide-open spaces were already getting crowded—well, relatively anyway. Besides the settlers, there were armies of soldiers bent on taming the native Americans and armies of laborers struggling to build the railroads. These railroads opened up the vast and dusty frontier to soft, pampered Easterners and Europeans anxious to grab some of the seemingly unlimited land. It was a slow, inexorable migration west. And just like Darwin taught us, it all came down to the survival of the fittest. In those days, staying alive meant one thing and only one thing: beef. To eat beef before the benefit of refrigerated transport, you needed live cattle. Since most of the cattle were in Texas and most of the hungry hordes were farther north (and, for a while, farther east), someone had to figure out how to get the beef off the hoof and onto their dinner plates. It was a lucrative business, but far from easy. In 1865, a Texas longhorn steer (the tough and leathery indigenous breed that reigned before selective breeding softened him up) cost $4 in Texas; in Kansas City or St. Louis he might fetch $40. The only problem was, the trek was 1,500 miles or more and walking was the only option.

This is where the cowboy came in. Although Mexican and Spanish vaqueros had been herding and branding cattle in the area for generations, they'd never had reason to transport them over such vast distances. Cowboys were a tough group of loners and misfits, many of whom had drifted west after the end of the Civil War. In fact, about 15 percent were probably African-Americans who first learned to handle cattle as slaves. As freed men, they sought their futures on the tough frontier, where a man's skill with a rope was more important than the color of his skin. Add a generous helping of true Mexican vaqueros, who brought their finely tooled leatherwork, saddles, and traditional boots into the mix, and a smattering of young, impoverished British aristocrats eager for adventure, and we begin to see that the group was distinctly "multi-cultural," even by today's standards. What drew this eclectic group together was their pride in and talent for their work, their rugged individuality, and of course, their outfits.

I see by your outfit that you are a cowboy:
You see by my outfit that I am one, too;
We see by our outfits that we are both cowboys;
Why'ncha get an outfit and be a cowboy too.

—Little-known verse of "The Streets of Laredo"

This book takes the tough, gritty cowboy tradition and turns it to the crucial task of creating cutting-edge cocktails. Today, the denizens of the cattle country might pull their chuck wagons behind a pick-up truck (or better yet, an SUV) and drink their whiskey cold, but the rough-and-tumble, dog-eat-dog atmosphere can still be felt in today's Wild West. Today's urban cowboys, and cowgirls, need a good cocktail to put a soft edge on a hard day, and in this book we've assembled the finest selections the West has ever seen. Paying homage to the cowboy's best friend (besides his horse), there are coffee-based cocktails that'll perk you up and wind you down at the same time. A chapter titled "Drinks from the Border" salutes the intense and ubiquitous influence of Mexico on the whole wranglin' tradition, and on Texas specifically. Cutting a little closer to true cowboy drinkin' tradition, a passel of shots and shooters will appeal to the dusty, swaggering cowboy in all of us. And for those who wouldn't dream of getting a speck of dirt on their brand-new Justin boots or white Stetson, we've collected a civilized selection of sophisticated sippers that would be right at home in the penthouse of a Fort Worth high-rise.

In "Quenchers from the Garden," we explore the mythical relationship between fruit flavors and strong spirits. After all, it was the pairing of limes and tequila that began one of the most lasting traditions of Southwest mixology, the margie. Finally, since everyone who's ever spent a long day on the trail winds up home in a dusty, bone-tired frame of mind, we've thoughtfully provided some smooth and soothing libations that are perfect for that moment when the sun reaches down to kiss the horizon.

Since a responsible drinker always keeps a full stomach to ward off the frightening effects of excessive alcohol intake (and, more to the point, since a drink often causes us to "put on the feed-bag"), you'll find "Tasty Vittles," a chapter full of salty, smoky, and fresh appetizers and nibbles that can be whipped up in two shakes.

And there's also the Cowboy Cocktails Reading Room, to help you get into the proper frame of mind for quaffing cowboy cocktails (don't miss *Cowboys Are My Weakness,* by Pam Houston). For the appropriate evening's entertainment with friends, you can browse through the Cowboy Cocktails Movie Thee-ater (we recommend you start off with *Giant,* with Rock Hudson, Liz Taylor, and James Dean—Reata restaurants are named for the ranch in this big, brash, totally Texas movie).

When setting out to write this book, we were sometimes asked "What's a cowboy cocktail?"

The answer is, it's not a drink—it's an attitude. We hope you'll adopt the attitude and get as much enjoyment out of sampling the recipes in this book as we had putting them together.

The Cowboy Cocktails Liquor Cabinet

SPIRITS

Amaretto
Bailey's Irish Cream
Blue Curaçao
Bourbon
Chambord
Cognac
Crème de Cacao
Crème de Menthe (green and white)
Frangelico
Gin
Goldschlager
Irish Whiskey: Bushmills or Jamesons
Kahlua
Mescal
Midori (melon liqueur)
Rum: white, spiced, 151
Rumpleminze
Schnapps:
    cinnamon, peach, butterscotch
Southern Comfort
Tia Maria
Tequila: Herradura white and gold
Triple Sec
Tuaca (honey-herb liqueur)
Vodka: Citrus, Tito's Texas, Stoli Vanil
Whiskey: Canadian, Irish, rye
Wild Turkey

WEAKER SPIRITS

Beer: Lone Star and Coors Light
Dry vermouth
Fruity red wine (such as Zinfandel)

WEAKER SPIRITS, cont.

Hard cider
Sparkling wine

REGALIA

Angostura bitters
Cinnamon, ground
Cloves, ground
Club soda
Cola
Cranberry juice
Dairy products:
    half-and-half, heavy cream
Dr Pepper
Ginger ale
Grapefruit juice (fresh)
Grenadine
Lemon juice (fresh)
Limes
Mint (fresh)
Orange juice (fresh)
Pineapple juice
Pineapple, canned
Sprite
Sugar, granulated and superfine
Tabasco, green
Tabasco, red
Tea
Tomato juice
Vanilla beans
Welch's grape juice

Techniques and Measurements

TECHNIQUES

Chilling glasses: When the instructions say to "chill a glass," that doesn't mean you have to place it in the freezer and wait thirty minutes. When you're ready for a cocktail, you're ready! Instead, simply fill the glass with ice and stir the ice twenty times in a circle (a chopstick is ideal for this operation). Let stand while you make the cocktail, and when it's ready, dump out the ice and replace it with the ice-cold cocktail itself—no need to dry the glass. Of course, if you have great powers of anticipation and simply "know" you'll be wanting a cocktail in the evening, you can place the glass(es) in the freezer in the morning before you leave for work (just after feeding the dog is good for us).

Rolling limes: At the famous La Floridita bar in Havana, Cuba, maestro bartender from 1912 to 1952 Constante Ribailagua employed a bar back (assistant) purely for the purpose of rolling his limes prior to squeezing them. A rolled lime will yield more juice, possibly as much as 30 percent more, so the practice bears repeating. Since limes around the country range from small and hard to large, luscious, and yielding, you'll have to decide if and how much rolling is indicated. If you are squeezing vast quantities of limes for a large event, count between 1 and $1^1/_2$ ounces of juice for each lime called for in the cocktail recipe. The technique is simple: roll the whole lime back and forth on the countertop, pressing down quite firmly with the palms of your hands. Five to ten seconds should be adequate. Then cut in half and squeeze as usual.

Floating: To "float," pour each individual liquor (if more than one is called for) very slowly over the back of an inverted teaspoon held about a half inch above the surface of the drink.

Salting or sugaring the rim of a glass: Fill a saucer with either salt or sugar, depending on the cocktail, to a depth of $^1/_8$ inch. Moisten the rim of the glass with lime, lemon, or any liquid that will be in the finished cocktail. Invert the glass in question and dip the rim into the salt or sugar. Twist back and forth a few times to make sure the crystals adhere. Gently turn the glass right-side up and pour in the cocktail.

Squeezing citrus juice: There are many contraptions available for extracting juice from the fresh limes, lemons, and oranges that should always be present in any good bartender's set-up. They range from a sharp-ended metal spout that is meant to be inserted into the fruit (squeeze and the juice comes pouring out? We don't think so—they are worse than useless), to reamer attachments for large food processors and standing mixers. Somewhere in between is where you'll most likely end up, with either a simple manual or electric reamer. Several models are available; choose one with a receptacle that will hold at least some of the juice. If you plan to serve a fair quantity of cocktails that require fresh lime juice, you'll want some sort of simple electric juicer, unless you have a need to contract instant arthritis.

MEASUREMENTS

1 pony	=	1 ounce, 2 tablespoons
1 jigger (shot)	=	$1^1/_2$ to 3 ounces, 3 to 6 tablespoons
1 dash	=	$^1/_6$ teaspoon
1 teaspoon	=	$^1/_8$ ounce
1 tablespoon	=	$^1/_2$ ounce

1

COWBOY COFFEE DRANKS

or a cowboy on the open range, coffee was like life's blood. Breakfast, lunch, dinner, and just shootin' the breeze—all were accompanied by steaming hot coffee no matter what the weather. Most cowboys slept rough, that is, they "used their bellies as a cover and their backs as a mattress." After a long, hard day (and a sometimes wet, cold night), coffee injected the vigor into their sluggish limbs and set them up for another day's ropin', brandin', and wranglin'. I think many of us today know exactly how they felt (whether we're ropin' a hot stock or wranglin' an eighteen-wheeler).

But cowboy coffee bore little resemblance to today's refined brews. For one thing, the grounds were not strained out. There was plenty of gear for the camp cook to manhandle without messing with filters and stuff—especially when you could just throw the grounds in the pot and boil it all up. Real cowboys had no time and less respect for weak coffee—they wanted coffee thick enough to eat with a fork. Thick, strong coffee gave a cowboy cast-iron innards and made him lively as a barefoot boy in a cactus patch. These tasty creations may be just dandy for today's urban and drugstore cowboys, but a real cowboy'd probably say they're as useless as a milk bucket under a bull and as weak as a two-day-old kitten. But don't let that stop you—some of these concoctions will knock you right off your horse.

Boquillas Border Coffee

Serves 1

Coffee was probably first mixed with spirituous drink in the famed "Irish Coffee," incidentally the only beverage that contains all four essential food groups in a single glass: alcohol, caffeine, sugar, and fat. This variation from the border still does the job nutrition-wise, but is much more to our liking flavor-wise.

> **6 or 7 ounces freshly brewed black coffee, pipin' hot**
> **$1^1/_2$ ounces Jose Cuervo Tequila**
> **1 tablespoon sugar**
> **1 tablespoon Kahlua Cream (page 127)**

Pour the hot coffee into a 12-ounce footed coffee glass. Add the tequila and sugar and stir until the sugar is dissolved. Garnish with the Kahlua cream. Olé!

RECOMMENDED LISTENING
"Another Cup of Coffee,"
by Cowboy Mouth,
from *Word of Mouth*

"It don't take near as much water to make coffee as some folks think it does."

—from *Western Words*
by Ramon F. Adams

Drugstore Cowboy Shake

Serves 4

Drugstore cowboys, or "dudes," are wannabe cowboys who may have the outfit, and may even talk the talk, but in general have never been closer to a cow than a T-bone steak. It may be a derogatory term from a dyed-in-the-wool cowhand, but if this luscious drink is your reward you'll likely get over the shame quicker than a dog who's heard his pan rattle.

4 cups freshly brewed black coffee, cooled to room temperature
6 ounces Bailey's Irish Cream
4 Cinnamon Stars (page 129)
Whipped cream, for garnish (sweeten the cream slightly with granulated sugar, if desired)
Coffee beans, for garnish

Chill four highball glasses until frosted. In a blender half-filled with ice, combine the coffee and the Bailey's and blend until smooth. Quickly pour into the chilled glasses and garnish with the cinnamon stars, whipped cream, and coffee beans. Mmmm, mmmm good.

RECOMMENDED LISTENING
"I Wanna Be a Cowboy,"
by Boys Don't Cry,
from *Club Mix-The 80's*

Vaquero Breakfast

Serves 2

Another variation on the lip-smacking tequila-Kahlua-coffee theme, this one's a little bit tamer. (Great for those mornings when your very own vaquero, or vaquera, requires help rollin' out of the sack.) Fry up a mess of "aigs" dirty on both sides, sizzle some bacon, and holler: "Roll out, roll out while she's hot! Bacon in the pan, coffee in the pot; Git up an' get it; Git it while it's hot." You will, undoubtedly, provoke some sort of reaction.

> 2 cups freshly brewed black coffee, pipin' hot
> $1^1/_4$ ounces tequila
> $^3/_4$ ounce Kahlua
> 2 tablespoons sugar

Pour 1 cup of the hot coffee into each of two 12-ounce footed coffee glasses. Divide the tequila, Kahlua, and sugar evenly among the glasses and stir until the sugar is completely dissolved. Serve immediately.

VARIATION: In the dog days of summer, stir the sugar into the coffee, cool, then serve this concoction over ice for a shiverin' wake up.

RECOMMENDED LISTENING
"Clouds in My Coffee,"
by Bonnie Tyler,
from *Silhouette in Red*

Fishin' with a Worm

Serves 1

The next time you and your pals are camped out at the local rio and wake up feeling the effects of the night before in a particularly unpleasant way, try this sharpener to put the hat straight on the day. If you're feeling as poor as a toothless coyote, use the garden-variety mescal that comes with the worm— otherwise spring for one of the super-premiums like Del Maguey. Either way, this one'll bite down hard and clear your head.

6 or 7 ounces freshly brewed black coffee, pipin' hot
1 ounce mescal (worm optional)

In a 12-ounce footed coffee glass, combine the coffee and the mescal and stir briefly. Sip till you feel a bite.

RECOMMENDED LISTENING
"Black Coffee-Drinkin' Woman,"
by Johnny B. Moore,
from *911 Blues*

SERVING HOT DRINKS:

Warning! Be sure to use tempered glassware. The footed glass coffee mugs seen in bars are preferable, but any tempered glass mug will do. Don't serve hot coffee drinks in metal, even if you're on the trail with only a tin cup—it just might burn your lips.

A Night on the Rio Grande

Serves 2

This slightly more refined libation is perfect for a romantic evening. Whether it's the Rio Grande, the Thames, or the East River you're feasting your peepers on, this drink really shines if served by moonlight. And, as they say in Texas, love may not make the world go round, but it sure makes the trip a whole lot more pleasant.

> **2 cups freshly brewed black coffee, pipin' hot**
> **1¹/₂ ounces Del Maguey Mezcal**
> **1¹/₂ ounces Triple Sec**

Pour 1 cup of the hot coffee into each of two 12-ounce footed coffee glasses. Divide the Mezcal and Triple Sec evenly among the glasses and stir to mix. Serve before the river rises.

RECOMMENDED LISTENING
"Moon Country,"
by Nat Gonella and His Georgians,
from *Georgia on My Mind*

"Two cowboys were eating a meal in a restaurant. One said, "The butter's so strong it could walk over and say howdy to the coffee." His pal answered, "Well, if it did, the coffee's too weak to answer back."
—from *Texas Traditions*
by Ross Phares

Alpine Latte

Serves 1

*Sweet, soothing, and smooth as a baby's bottom.
Don't even mention this one to your favorite cowhand ("Frangeli-WHAT?!").*

$^1/_2$ ounce Bailey's Irish Cream

1 ounce amaretto

1 ounce Frangelico

6 or 7 ounces freshly brewed coffee,
   pipin' hot

Whipped cream, for garnish (sweeten the cream
   slightly with granulated sugar, if desired)

Chopped almonds, for garnish

In a 12-ounce footed coffee glass, combine the Bailey's, amaretto, and
Frangelico. Add the coffee and stir once. Garnish with the whipped
cream and almonds, and sip, don't gulp.

RECOMMENDED LISTENING
"Black Coffee,"
by Sonny Criss,
from *This Is Criss!*

Southern Cross

Serves 1

The Southern Cross was one of the first big ranches in Texas, and it was owned by an Irishman (hence the ingredients of this cocktail). When we say "big," we are talking millions of acres. Those first ranches were so big they were like a country unto themselves, and many ranchers referred to their ranches as their "country," as in: "I'm going over to Bick's country," or "Get that herd of sheep out of my country." The Tia Maria and Kahlua here add a touch of old Mexico, reflecting the hybrid style that soon overtook Irishmen and all the other immigrants who set out in the mid 1800s to make the territory of "Tejas" their own.

> **1 ounce traditional Irish whiskey (such as Bushmills or Jameson)**
> **Splash of Tia Maria**
> **6 or 7 ounces freshly brewed coffee, pipin' hot**
> **2 tablespoons Kahlua Cream (page 127)**

In a 12-ounce footed coffee glass, combine the whiskey, Tia Maria, and coffee. Stir once, top with the Kahlua cream, and serve immediately.

RECOMMENDED LISTENING
Any track from *Wild Colonial Boy*,
by Glen Curtin

The law of "primogeniture" in the British Isles directed that the eldest son inherited an entire estate, while second and third sons were left with nothing but their stiff upper lips. As a consequence, many well-bred and ambitious young men were forced to leave Britain's shores to seek their fortunes in the New World. Lured by the romance and wide open spaces of the West, many set out to become cattle barons. We may be used to hearing John Wayne speak in a slow drawl as he wrangles a herd on the big screen, but many men of the Old West actually spoke with a more clipped accent— one that would be more at home in Dublin or Donegal than in Dodge City.

Spindletop

Serves 1

Widely misunderstood as being the first big gusher in Texas oil history, the Spindletop was actually an entire oil field. The well in question was Lucas No. 1, and on January 10, 1901, the well came in at 1,200 feet, spewing oil for 6 days at 75,000 barrels a day, before it could be successfully capped (that's a total of almost 19 million gallons, more than one and a half times the spill from the Exxon Valdez). Within a month, this one well exceeded Texas's oil production for the entire previous year. No wonder it's legendary (and think of the clean-up). This sophisticated coffee drink will become legendary at your own dining table with its subtle almond-cinnamon aroma and luscious cinnamon 'n' cream garnish.

> 1 ounce amaretto
> $^1/_2$ ounce Triple Sec
> 6 or 7 ounces freshly brewed coffee, pipin' hot
> Splash of cinnamon schnapps
> Whipped cream, for garnish (sweeten the cream slightly with
>   granulated sugar, if desired)
> Ground cinnamon, for garnish

In a 12-ounce footed coffee glass, combine the amaretto, Triple Sec, and coffee. Add the schnapps, stir once, and top with a tablespoon or two of whipped cream. Sprinkle the whipped cream with just a touch of cinnamon and serve.

RECOMMENDED LISTENING
"One More Last Dance,"
by Vince Gill,
from *Ultimate Country Party*

East Texas Mocha

Serves 1

For those who don't know Texas geography (don't despair, you can still learn), remember it's a big, big state. West Texas is down by the Mexico border and bears the indelible stamp of Old Mexico in talk, dress, food, and attitude. East Texas is over by Louisiana and feels the spicy influence of Creole and Cajun culture, hence the bourbon in this sweet, delicious froth. If you are a coffee-lover you probably have all the regalia, including a coffee machine with a little steamed milk wand. Otherwise, just bring some milk to a simmer in a small saucepan and skim off the froth—but watch out—hot milk boils over extremely quickly.

> 1 ounce bourbon
> 1 ounce Crème de Cacao
> 6 or 7 ounces freshly brewed coffee, pipin' hot
> Steamed milk, for garnish

In a 12-ounce footed coffee glass, combine the bourbon, Crème de Cacao, and coffee. Stir once. Top with a little steamed milk and serve.

RECOMMENDED LISTENING
"At the Chocolate Bon Bon Ball,"
by Leon Redbone,
from *Up a Lazy River*

"RECIPE FOR COWBOY COFFEE:

Take two pounds of Arbuckles coffee, put in 'nough water to wet it down, boil it for two hours, then throw in a hoss shoe. If the hoss shoe sinks, it ain't ready."

—from *Come an' Git It*,
by Ramon F. Adams

2

DRINKS FROM THE BORDER

exas and Mexico. Mexico and Texas. They go together like beans and cheese, like guys and trucks, like beer and tequila. One thing you can't deny: Texas and Mexico share a bond that runs wider than the Rio Grande. Admittedly, Mexican influence on Texas is a lot stronger than Texan influence on Mexico. Texas may be big, but there's a whole lot of power south of that border. A little thing called the Texas revolution separated the northern territory of "Tejas" from the country of Mexico back in 1836, after Colonel James Walker Fannin Jr. and four hundred brave men died defending the Alamo against a huge and fierce Mexican army. The Republic of Texas, an independent nation, lasted until 1845 when Texas joined the United States. It's no wonder Texans are proud and headstrong. As Sam Houston once said, "Texas could get along without the United States, but the United States cannot, except at great hazard, exist without Texas."

Listen to a conversation in any Texas town and it's likely that borrowed Mexican words will make up 30 percent of it. Ex-wife took all your money? She got "the whole enchilada." Gotta go? It's time to "vamoose." A modern cowboy could get up in the morning, grab his "lariat," ride up to the "mesa," "lasso" a cow, and finish out the day sippin' a "margarita."

Open a menu: Mexican food rules, hands down. Of course it's not *real* Mexican food. It's the hybrid "Tex-Mex"—mostly nachos, chili, fajitas, burritos, enchiladas, and plenty of jalapeños—all stuff that goes down real good with a cold beer (a Lone Star, preferably).

So, next time you're hankerin' after a festive evening, cue up Herb Alpert, ice down the shaker, and lasso your favorite 'lil dogies for a selection of Latin libations. Viva la Raza!

El Crudo

Serves 1

As you might expect, the lore of the West—both then and now—abounds with sure-fire antidotes for the dreaded hangover. This is a classic Texas remedy for "El Crudo" (slang for hangover). We advise that you vary the amount of Tabasco according to taste and the time of your first meeting of the day.

> Coarse or kosher salt
> 1 bottle Dos Equis lager beer
> 1 tablespoon freshly squeezed lime juice
> Dash of Tabasco, or to taste

Salt the rim of a chilled glass beer mug (see page 7). Fill the mug half way with ice. Pour the beer over the ice and add the lime juice and Tabasco. Drink quickly while keeping your head as still as possible.

RECOMMENDED LISTENING
"Ain't Going Down 'Til the Sun Comes Up,"
by Garth Brooks,
from *In Pieces*

Mezcal Margarita

Serves 1

The margarita may just be the most popular cocktail north or south of the border. There are more claims as to the originator of the legendary drink than hell has sinners, but even more fun than the original concoction is the sport of creating new 'ritas. This one'll really get the dog out from under the porch.

> 2 ounces Del Maguey Mezcal
> 2 ounces freshly squeezed lime juice
> 2 ounces Triple Sec
> 1¹/₂ ounces orange juice

Salt the rim of a large, chilled margarita glass (see page 7) and add a small scoop of crushed or broken ice. In a cocktail shaker half-filled with ice, combine all of the ingredients. Shake hard and fast, then immediately strain into the prepared glass. *Chingado!*

RECOMMENDED LISTENING
"Rock Esta Noche,"
by Joe "King" Carrasco,
from *Tex-Mex Rock-Roll*

Tequila and Mescal

If you're like us, there's no way you can remember if the saying goes, "All tequila is mescal, but not all mescal is tequila," or if it's the other way around. Here's the lowdown: Tequila, mescal, and pulque are the three most popular spirituous beverages in Mexico (after beer), and they all come from the fermented juice of same plant, the maguey, or agave (one close relative is known north of the border as the century plant). Tequila and mescal are then distilled, pulque is not. Pulque is about the same alcoholic strength as beer and has never been popular outside of Mexico, perhaps because it is sometimes described as having a flavor reminiscent of a mildewed donkey. To be fair, it is made only from the Giant Pulque Agave (only found in Mexico) and doesn't travel well (it loses its, ah, finesse within three to five days).

Of the three, tequila is best known to Norteamericaños and comes from a specific region and a special variety of maguey, the blue agave. Mescal also comes only from a specific region, which surrounds and includes the state of Oaxaca. Until recently, mescal has unfortunately been best known as "the bottle with the worm" and has caused the temporary demise of many a hardy partier in the Southwest (bottles often cost less than four dollars and came with a complimentary bag of seasoned salt—seasoned with pulverized maguey worms, that is). Recently, however, premium and super-premium mescals are being produced and have increased the quality level of mescal considerably. To make tequila, the heart of the agave plant is steamed before fermentation, but for mescal it is roasted, imparting the smoky flavor so beloved by connoisseurs. The organically produced, single-village mescals of Del Maguey stand head and shoulders above the crowd—each village's mescal has a unique flavor that comes from a variety of influences such as water, the local yeasts, microclimate, altitude, and of course, the hand of the maker. Flavors range from spicy and smoky to floral and smooth. Sipped alone, very slowly, or mixed into a cocktail, the flavor of premium mescal is difficult to describe but easy to fall for. (Don't sip too much or too fast, or you'll be falling down—straight mescal is strong enough to melt your tonsils, and premium or not, it doesn't taste any too special coming back up.)

Remember the Alamo

Serves 1

Surrounded, outgunned, and far outnumbered, the men who fell at the Alamo are Texas heroes, more revered even than the winning high school football team. Here, the lonesome Lone Star is similarly surrounded—this time by some of the best spirits Mexico has to offer. But in this case, you're more likely to want to make love, not war.

$1^1/_2$ **ounces tequila**
$1^1/_2$ **ounces Lone Star beer**
$1^1/_2$ **ounces premium mescal**

Fill three shot glasses with the separate ingredients. Quickly drink the tequila shot, then the Lone Star shot, then the mescal shot.

RECOMMENDED LISTENING
Pensive: "Ballad of the Alamo,"
by Marty Robbins,
from *More Greatest Hits;*
or upbeat: "Alamo Rag,"
by Adolf Hofner,
from *South Texas Swing*

Margtini

Serves 1

This sophisticated cocktail is a hybrid of two of the world's greatest drinks: the margarita and the martini. It's guaranteed to make your favorite urban cowgirl or cowboy happier than an armadillo diggin' grub worms.

> **1¹/₂ ounces premium tequila**
> **¹/₂ ounce Triple Sec**
> **Juice from 3 limes**
> **Splash of soda**

Salt the rim of a cocktail or small margarita glass (see page 7) and chill. In a cocktail shaker half-filled with ice, combine all of the ingredients. Shake hard and fast, then immediately strain into the chilled glass and serve.

RECOMMENDED LISTENING
"Mister Richard Smoker,"
by Ween,
from *Ween 12 Golden Country Greats*

COWBOY VOCABULARY:

"There's no back door to that Alamo."
Meaning: forget about it, you're sunk.

A Day in Boquillas

Serves 2 or more, depending on stamina

South of Big Bend National Park down in West Texas, there's a sleepy little border town called Boquillas. The only way to get there is to walk down to the river and hire the boatman to row you across. On the other side, you'll ride a donkey up to the village itself, which has no electricity but sports a fine (usually) generator for keeping the beer somewhat cold. The man to see about excellent grub is Jose Falcon—order his excellent little burritos or tacos (the only thing on the menu) by the half dozen or dozen. There's a fine, slow, and dusty party atmosphere in Boquillas. Discover the culture of this fine Mexican village . . . but don't drink the water.

Six-pack of your favorite beer
1 bottle cheap tequila

Sip and stroll. Repeat as desired, and kick up your heels at the consequences.

RECOMMENDED LISTENING
"Blame it On Mexico,"
by George Strait,
from *Strait out of the Box*

The Smoky Floater

"Floater" is a term that is fondly familiar to serious mixologists and devoted barflies. It means a final little splash of liquor, usually fairly strong, that is "floated" atop the finished cocktail just before it is served. If the right liquor is chosen, the effect is profound beyond expectation, imbuing the cocktail with a subtle hint of extra flavor and a lovely kick. Mark Miller entered one of his inventions, the "Smoking Margarita," in the First Annual Grand Margarita contest in Santa Fe, using Del Maguey's unique, smoky Mezcal Chichicapa as the final floater. Since then, those in-the-know routinely request a "smoky floater," ($1/2$ ounce Chichicapa) atop all their margaritas.

Reata 'Rita

Serves 1

This famous cocktail has fans from Fort Worth to Rodeo Drive and is a great option for days when you've run out of the bartender's best friend: fresh limes. It's so good it'll make you want to call your grandma and jaw for awhile!

> 1 $^3/_4$ ounces Herradura Silver Tequila
> 1 ounce orange juice
> 3 ounces Reata Sweet 'n' Sour Mix (page 128)
> $^1/_4$ ounce Triple Sec
> Wedge of lime, for garnish

Moisten the rim of a large glass tumbler (at Reata we use a 16-ouncer!) with lime juice and invert it in a dish of salt to frost the rim. Add a few large scoops of crushed or broken ice to the glass. In a cocktail shaker half-filled with ice, combine all of the ingredients except the lime. Shake hard and fast, then immediately strain into the prepared glass. Garnish the edge of the glass with the lime wedge and serve.

RECOMMENDED LISTENING
"The Good, The Bad, and The Ugly,"
by Hugo Montenegro,
from *Songs of the West, Vol. 4*

Bloody Maria

Serves 1

If your bigger half tends to sleep like a dead calf on Sunday mornings, waft this conversation juice under his nose a few times. He'll be up quicker than you can bat an eye. But watch out, 'cause before you know it he'll be hungry as a coyote with a toothache.

2 $^1/_2$ ounces tequila
5 ounces tomato juice
$^1/_2$ ounce freshly squeezed lemon juice
$^1/_8$ teaspoon black pepper
$^1/_8$ teaspoon celery salt
Dash of Tabasco sauce

In a cocktail shaker half-filled with ice, combine all of the ingredients. Shake hard and fast, then immediately strain into a double old-fashioned glass, over rocks, and serve.

RECOMMENDED LISTENING
"Tequila,"
by The Champs,
from *Tequila-Rockin' Instrumentals*

Border Crossing

Serves 1

This variation on the ever-popular Cuba Libre substitutes tequila for the rum and adds a bracing note of fresh citrus to the brew. Whether you're hoofing a dusty trail or working your abs poolside, this is a quencher to reckon with.

1^1/$_2$ ounces tequila
2 teaspoons freshly squeezed lime juice
1 teaspoon freshly squeezed lemon juice
4 ounces cola
Wedge of lime, for garnish

Place 4 to 6 ice cubes in a highball glass. Add the tequila, lime and lemon juices, and the cola. Stir well and garnish with the lime. Serve immediately, without looking back.

RECOMMENDED LISTENING
"Negra Traicion,"
by Flaco Jimenez,
from *Tex-Mex Conjunto Classics*

Cactus Bite

Serves 1

These days, anyone worth their salt-and-lemon knows that tequila comes from the fermented and distilled juice of the blue agave plant (well, most people do, don't they?). What many don't know, however, is that the agave is not a cactus, it's a member of the lily family. Certain marketers of certain tequilas seem content to let the public hold on to their misconception, probably because cactus juice sounds a lot more manly than lily juice.

> **2 ounces tequila**
> **2 teaspoons Cointreau**
> **2 teaspoons Drambuie**
> **2 ounces lemon juice**
> **$1/2$ teaspoon sugar**
> **Dash of Angostura bitters**

Chill a cocktail glass. In a cocktail shaker half-filled with ice, combine all the ingredients. Shake hard and fast, then immediately strain into the chilled glass and serve. Ouch!

RECOMMENDED LISTENING
"La Ratita,"
by Conjunto Alamo,
from *Tex-Mex Fiesta*

Yellow Rose of Texas

Serves 1

If you like your cocktails on the gentle side, this warm-hued libation will have you purrin' like a kitten in a creamery. And if you like a little history with your drankin', you'll want to know that the Yellow Rose of Texas isn't a flower, she was a girl—a Texas slave girl named Emily Morgan to be exact. She caught the eye of Mexican general Santa Anna and caused him to lose the thread, just slightly, of what he was supposed to be doing (attacking the Texas army at San Jacinto in 1836—we all know how that can be, right?). Whether or not she "caught his eye" on purpose is not known, but while he was distracted the Texas army defeated his forces and led the territory to victory and independence. She's since been immortalized in a song that's sung from one end of the state to the other.

> 2 ounces orange juice
> 1 ounce Southern Comfort
> $^1/_2$ ounce premium tequila

In a cocktail shaker half-filled with ice, combine all of the ingredients. Shake hard and fast, then immediately strain into an old-fashioned glass, over rocks, and serve.

RECOMMENDED LISTENING
"Corina, Corina,"
by Freddie Fender,
from *Tex-Mex Fiesta*

Park Kerr, founder of the El Paso Chile Company, knows a thing or two about entertaining Texas-style. In addition to producing some mighty tasty sauces, salsas, and snacks, he is now making his own tequila from one hundred percent blue agave. Tequila Nacional is fermented in small batches to yield an exquisite silver tequila, crisp and sweetly alive. Kerr's shimmering revelation is right at home with any cowboy cocktail that calls for tequila.

3

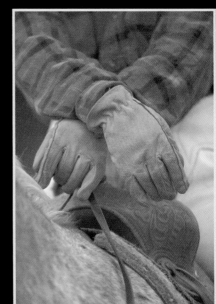

SHOTS AND SHOOTERS

Three

Short, sweet, and straight to the point—that's how a cowboy likes his work, his women, and his liquor. These shots and shooters are true to the prairie tradition, with a few modern twists thrown in, of course. Since there's not much in a shot except the liquor itself, the liquor should be good, and it should be cold. For best results, always keep good liquor in the freezer, especially tequila.

Shooters have become popular with the college crowd, who presumably don't have the time or the resources to set up a full bar with all the shakers, mixers, measuring devices, and strainers that the older generations have recently become re-enamored with. A shooter can still have some class, however, depending on what it goes down with and how (like a dash of Tabasco, a sprinkle of pepper, or followed by a beer).

Remember that back in the day, the quintessential "cowboy cocktail" was a shot of whiskey in a dirty glass. It might have been home brew, rot gut, or "panther piss," but to a thirsty cowboy, a shot of whiskey was as welcome as a pardon to a lifer. As lonely as the cowboys were, getting together over a dirty glass and a bottle was likely to mean a lot of jawing. It's been said of many a cowboy, "He ain't exactly tongue-tied when it comes to makin' chin music" (hence the term "Conversation Fluid" for whiskey). Today's urban cowboys and cowgirls are more likely to be afflicted with the "D and D's" (drinkin' and dialin').

Trail Dust

Serves 1

Don't get caught riding drag when this concoction is being poured up. We like to make this one with a "dirty rim," a variation of the salt rim found on the margarita: First, pour some Demerara raw sugar into a saucer that is wider than the diameter of the glass; run a slice of lemon around the rim of the glass, then invert the glass and twist back and forth in the sugar until the rim is coated.

> **1 ounce El Tesoro White Tequila**
> **1 ounce whiskey**
> **Pinch of black pepper**

In a cocktail shaker one-quarter filled with ice cubes, combine the tequila, whiskey, and black pepper. Shake hard and fast, then strain into a Texas jigger or a small old-fashioned glass. Serve immediately. (If desired, you can serve this drink on the rocks.) Drink quickly and then mop your brow with the closest thing you have to a bandana.

RECOMMENDED LISTENING
"I Think I'll Just Stay Here and Drink,"
by Merle Haggard & the Strangers,
from *Western Swing, Various Artists*

Lust in the Dust (or Strawberry Roan)

Serves 1

If your nose should come into conflict with the pickled pepper while sipping this icy-hot cocktail, simply remove the pepper from the glass and eat it. That'll stop the durned thing from getting in your way. Don't even think of omitting the pepper—that's a sissy drink. Shaking this cocktail with ice makes it technically a cocktail rather than a shooter, but it also combines the vodka with the Tabasco much more efficiently. And, as a bonus, you get the little shimmering shards of ice that slip through the strainer if you shake it nice and hard.

> **2 ounces premium vodka, chilled**
> **1 teaspoon Tabasco, or to taste**
> **Pickled Jalapeño Pepper (page 130), for garnish**

Chill a small cocktail glass or an old-fashioned glass. In a cocktail shaker one-quarter filled with ice, combine the vodka and Tabasco. Shake hard and fast then immediately strain into the chilled glass. Garnish with the pickled pepper and serve.

RECOMMENDED LISTENING
"Switchin' in the Kitchen,"
by Asleep at the Wheel,
from *Asleep at the Wheel*

West Texas Tequila Slammer

Serves 1

Whenever we hear the term "slammer" applied to a drink, we imagine some saloon patron slamming his drink down hard on the bar while trying to score a conversational point, or just get the bartender's attention. Either way, the term sums up visions of a real Western bar brawl, not a very pleasant experience in person, perhaps, but plenty appealing when staged for film. (For a Hollywood-inspired, hopped-up version of a Wild West saloon brawl, check out Tony Curtis, Natalie Wood, Jack Lemmon, Peter Falk, Keenan Wynn, and Larry Storch in the so-hokey-it's-good movie The Great Race, *made in 1965.)*

> **1¹/₂ ounces tequila, thoroughly chilled**
> **Dash of Tabasco**
> **Splash of club soda**

Combine the tequila and Tabasco in a large shot glass or an old-fashioned glass. Add a splash of soda. Cover the glass with one hand and slam the glass down on the table or bar. Drink while it's still fizzing and everyone's still lookin' atcha.

RECOMMENDED LISTENING
"I Guess I Was Buzzed,"
by The Groovy Rednecks,
from *Buzzed*

Silver Bullet

Serves 1

For many years in West Texas, the only two beers available were Lone Star and Coors Light, which accounts for what many consider a slightly "sissy" beer in this manly concoction.

> 1¹/₂ ounces Patron Silver Tequila, well chilled
> 1 bottle Coors Light, ice cold

Pour the tequila into a standard shot glass. Drink the shot and quickly chase with a swig of Coors Light. Repeat as necessary. Oh, and by the way, boys don't cry.

RECOMMENDED LISTENING
"There's a Tear in My Beer,"
by Hank Williams,
from *Complete Hank Williams, Sr.*

COWBOY VOCABULARY
TO DRINK, IN TEXAS:

VERB, present: *drank*, as in "Ah ain't gonna *drank* that—it's water!"
VERB, past: *drank*, as in "Merle done *drank* up all the Lone Stars, durn it!"
VERB, past perfect: *drank*, as in "We was gonna *drank* that iced tea, honey, but Merle brought some whiskey, instead."

Red-Haired Turkey Shoot

Serves 1

The Tabasco settles gently into this premium American bourbon, looking for all the world like thin strands of red hair settling down through the spirits. Ideally, find a red-headed partner to drink this with (we know of some mighty nice ones from Texas—must be all that Irish blood).

> **1¹/₂ ounces Wild Turkey, preferably well chilled**
> **Dash of Tabasco, or to taste**

Pour the Wild Turkey into a shot glass. Add a dash or two of Tabasco and drink before you change your mind.

RECOMMENDED LISTENING
"Cleopatra, Queen of Denial,"
by Pam Tillis,
from *Greatest Hits*

COWBOY VOCABULARY
TO DRINK, IN TEXAS:

NOUN, singular: *Drank*, as in "Could ah git a *drank*, here, or whuut?"
NOUN, plural: *Dranks*, as in "Me and Merle got a few *dranks* down on the corner."

Texas Prairie Fire

Serves 1

It took a lot to scare a real cowboy, but a fire on the prairie could cause the blood of the toughest cowhand to run ice cold (most of them were caused by a stray bolt of lightning). Cows might seem slow and stupid, but a few hundred running for their lives from a fire can wreak the most frightening kind of destruction. This little drink is bigger than it sounds and will light a fire in your belly that won't go out till you drink another one. After that, it's every man for hisself. **Note:** *True Texans will know of another kind of prairie fire: the renowned and revered refried bean dip from Texas über-store Nieman Marcus.*

> ³/₄ **ounce tequila, very cold**
> ¹/₂ **ounce freshly squeezed lime juice**
> **Dash or two of green Tabasco**

Combine all the ingredients in a shot glass and serve immediately, before you get burned. **Note:** green Tabasco is made from jalapeño peppers and is available in well-stocked markets and liquor stores.

RECOMMENDED LISTENING
"80-Proof Bottle of Tear-Stopper,"
by George Strait,
from *Strait Out of the Box*

Branding Iron

Serves 1

Several hours before you plan to concoct this little hotty, place both the tequila and the rumpleminze in the freezer. Perfect after a hard day's work in the fields or on the trading floor.

> **1¹/₂ ounces white tequila, well chilled**
> **1 ounce rumpleminze or peppermint schnapps, well chilled**

Chill a large shot glass or a small old-fashioned glass. Pour the tequila and rumpleminze into the chilled glass and stir once with a swizzle stick. Serve pronto, and keep some ice water handy to put out any fires.

RECOMMENDED LISTENING
"John Doe on a John Deere,"
by Lonestar,
from *Crazy Nights*

TEXAS BUMPER STICKERS:

"Hell yes I'm drunk—What do you think I am, a stunt driver?"

The Texican

Serves 1

*Town names in the South are often made up
of two places combined: Texarkana, Mexicali,
etc. (The oil company Texaco, however, is not a
combination of Texas and Mexico but rather
Texas and "Co.") The Texican brings together a
Texas favorite with a Mexican must. South of the
border, cranberry juice is not a common sight—
while north of the border the Cosmopolitan has
claimed many a lady's heart. Make your Cosmo
the Texican way—with tequila—and we think you'll
be converted for life.*

1¹/₄ **ounces tequila**
2 **ounces cranberry juice**
1 **teaspoon freshly squeezed lime juice**
Thin slice of lime, for garnish

In a cocktail shaker one-quarter filled with ice, combine the tequila,
cranberry juice, and lime juice. Shake hard and fast, then immediately
strain into an old-fashioned glass straight up or over ice. Garnish with
the lime slice and serve.

RECOMMENDED LISTENING
"Did I Shave My Legs for This?"
by Deana Carter,
from *Did I Shave My Legs for This?*

Irish Cowboy

Serves 1

Even Irishmen on the range stay true to Irish whiskey no matter what the years may have blown their way. This smooth drink brings the best of Ireland to your living room—with a little color for the patriotic amongst ye. After all, Saint Patrick's Day is always just around the corner—isn't it now?

> 1¹/₂ ounces Irish whiskey
> 1 tablespoon Bailey's Irish Cream
> 1 tablespoon crème de menthe

Chill a large shot glass or a small old-fashioned glass. In a cocktail shaker half-filled with ice, combine all the ingredients. Shake hard and fast, then immediately strain into the chilled glass. Serve at once, with or without the blarney.

RECOMMENDED LISTENING
"Broken Whiskey Glass,"
by Jason and The Scorchers,
from *Lost & Found*

Cowboy Vocabulary: **Names for Horses**

Cowboys were a lonely breed, and by necessity spent a lot of time with their horses. Cowboy poetry abounds with references to horses—old, young, ornery, and devoted. A horse to a cowboy was something like a wife. In fact, many cowboys had a sort of love-hate relationship with their horses, as evidenced by this list of slang names for horses:

Bangtail	Calf Horse	Gotch-Ear	Knothead
Boneyard	Carvin' Horse	Gut Twister	Man Killer
Bronco	Cayuse	Hammerhead	Nag
Broomtail	Choppin' Horse	Hay Burner	Plug
Bucker	Circle Horse	Indian Digger	Ringtail
Buzzard Bait	Fantail	Jughead	Shavetail

Cowboy Vocabulary: **Names for Whiskey**

When a group of people has a lot of names for something, it usually means that "something" is pretty important to their lifestyle. Witness the Eskimos, who, depending on the authority you consult, have either twenty-four or several hundred different names for snow. And witness the (far from exhaustive) list below of cowboy terms for spirited beverages:

Barleycorn	Conversation	Liquid Dynamite	Red Eye
Base Burner	Fluid	Liquid Fire	Rot Gut
Boose	Fire Water	Moonshine	Scamper Juice
Bouse	Grog	Neck Oil	Snake Poison
Brave Maker	Gut Warmer	Nose Paint	Swill
Bug Juice	Home Brew	Panther Piss	Tarantula Juice
Coffin Varnish	Hooch	Pottle	Tonsil Varnish

4

SIPPIN' WITH THE CITY SLICKERS

he cowboy tradition in today's Texas is far from dead—in fact, you'd be surprised how many real cowboys are still around. True, a certain percentage of these are just drugstore cowboys, dudes, and plain old wannabes. And lots of the real cowhands that *are* left are off beyond the horizon, working the dusty arroyos, and tending to what they've always tended to: cows. You just can't see them from the highway.

In the big towns of the Southwest there are plenty of cowboy hats and even more boots in evidence, but that doesn't necessarily make the wearers cowboys. More likely, they're just city slickers. When you're in the mood for some creative tippling, though, these slickers are the bodies to find. That's 'cause wherever they are, the drinkin' and chow's likely to be good. Rest your Stetson on the leather bar, then choose from some liquored-up libations no real cowboy would be seen dead drinking (but it don't hardly matter cause you're not a real cowboy anyway).

There's little doubt that the renaissance of the cocktail culture in the late 90s has led to some questionable concoctions (we won't mention any by name in case they're your personal favorites). But some of the new cocktails contain the seeds of true greatness—and we think we have quite a selection ra-cheer (that's "right here," as pronounced in Texas). It was the resurgence of the classic martini that, arguably, led the stampede, and one by-product of that popularity has been the addition of the postscript "-tini" to any newly created cocktail. It may be silly, but it's definitely fun, and who're we to buck a trend (see the Fruitini on page 52 for one of our very best).

Well Water

Serves 2

Cool as a breeze off the night prairie, blue as a Texas cheerleader's eyes, and deep as the ocean. That's the way we like our wells to come in, and that's the way we like this neon-blue refresco, too. Stirring instead of the usual shaking makes this cocktail crystal clear, with no ice shards to obscure the view.

3 ounces Gilbey's Gin, chilled
2 ounces Triple Sec, chilled
1 ounce Blue Curaçao
Crushed ice

Chill two cocktail glasses. In a mixing glass half-filled with crushed ice, combine all the ingredients. Stir well, but gently, and strain into the chilled glasses. Drink long and deep—who knows when you'll pass this way again.

RECOMMENDED LISTENING
"Blue Water,"
by Poco,
from *Crazy Eyes*

Texas Cosmopolitan

Serves 1

The only thing that makes this a Texas Cosmo is that Tito's Texas vodka, made in Austin, replaces the usual bar brands. There's a reason the Cosmopolitan has taken the country by storm in our recent cocktail-mania—it's a truly great drink! If you'd like it a little sweeter, increase the Triple Sec.

> 1³/₄ ounces Tito's Texas vodka
> ¹/₄ ounce Triple Sec
> Splash of cranberry juice
> Wedge of lime, for garnish

Chill a Texas jigger or a small cocktail glass. In a cocktail shaker half-filled with ice, combine the vodka, Triple Sec, and cranberry juice. Shake hard and fast, then strain into the chilled glass. Perch the lime wedge on the edge of the glass and serve at once, this very momen-*tito*.

RECOMMENDED LISTENING
"Quiche Woman in a Barbecue Town,"
by Clyde Edgerton,
from *Walking Across Egypt*

COWBOY VOCABULARY:

Dude: A Rexall ranger, or drugstore cowboy, as in "The only horse that dude ever had was a charley horse."

Fruitini

Serves 1

As with most of the cocktails in this chapter, a real cowboy'd be likely to take one look at this drink and hot-foot it towards the hills. But there's something truly special about the combo of fiery, smoky mescal and that fruity, feminine peach schnapps. This colorful concoction may earn itself a warm place in your heart.

1¼ ounces Manero mescal
¼ ounce peach schnapps
1 ounce freshly squeezed orange juice
Thin slice of orange, for garnish

Chill a small cocktail glass. In a cocktail shaker half-filled with ice, combine the mescal, schnapps, and orange juice. Shake hard and fast and strain into the chilled glass. Perch the orange slice on the edge of the glass and serve before you can say "picking peaches in peachtree plaza."

RECOMMENDED LISTENING
"Georgia Peaches,"
by Pirates of the Mississippi,
from *Walk the Plank*

Cancuntini

Serves 1

In a cocktail like this where the pineapple flavor stars, be sure to use a white tequila—gold tequilas are full of colorings and caramel that will interfere with the clean, smooth flavor of this simple drink. When there are only a few ingredients, it's essential that each one be of the best quality available. So it goes without saying that fresh pineapple juice will make this drink stand out like a Stetson in a crowd of baseball caps. Head for the nearest beach or pool with your shaker in tow! For the fashion-conscious among you, we recommend a pineapple beach towel and, for the ladies, pineapple earrings (what you wear as a sun-hat is up to you—but remember Carmen Miranda!).

> 1 ounce white tequila
> 1 ounce Triple Sec
> 1 ounce pineapple juice
> 1 teaspoon grenadine syrup
> Wedge of pineapple, for garnish

Chill a cocktail glass. In a cocktail shaker half-filled with ice, combine the tequila, Triple Sec, pineapple juice, and grenadine. Shake hard and fast, then immediately strain into the chilled glass. Garnish with a pineapple wedge and serve right quick.

Note: Stemmed plastic cocktail glasses are available in several colors and sizes and benefit greatly from being frozen down, even for just a few minutes. We have a rule about plastic glasses at pool-side that has saved our hearts from much potential achy-breakage.

RECOMMENDED LISTENING
"South American Way,"
by Carmen Miranda,
from *The Brazilian Bombshell*

Five-Card Draw

Serves 1

Real men and real card players may drink bourbon neat, but real people often want a little flavor and a little smoothness to complement the bite. Spiced rum adds an exotic flavor here that will have you thinkin' you've just blustered your way into the hottest game in New Orleans. Be sure to sit facing the door so's you can't be taken by surprise.

$1^1/_2$ **ounces bourbon**
$^1/_2$ **ounce Bacardi Spiced Rum**
Splash of half-and-half

In a cocktail shaker half-filled with ice, combine the bourbon and the rum. Shake hard and fast, then immediately strain into a Texas Jigger or an old-fashioned glass over rocks. Drizzle on the half-and-half and serve without peeking at anybody's cards.

RECOMMENDED LISTENING
"Darktown Poker Club,"
by Phil Harris,
from *My Kind of Country*

Texas Widebrim

Serves 2

This is our special twist on the Sombrero, a cocktail that is rich in Mexican history. It's sweet as a grandmother's kiss and slick as a watermelon seed— definitely the choice for those with a sweet tooth. Don't keep it under your hat—remember the wisdom of the Old West: "Share and share alike." We like to sip this after dinner with some pungent peppermints on the side.

> **1 ounce Bailey's Irish Cream**
> **1 ounce amaretto**
> **2 ounces half-and-half**
> **$^1/_2$ ounce Bacardi 151 Rum**
> **Kahlua Cream (page 127), for garnish**

Chill two Texas jiggers or old-fashioned glasses. In a blender, combine 10 ice cubes with the Bailey's, amaretto, half-and-half, and rum. Blend until smooth and pour into the chilled glasses. Garnish with dollops of the Kahlua cream. Tip your hat and remember to serve the ladies first.

RECOMMENDED LISTENING
"Don't Touch My Hat,"
by Lyle Lovett,
from *Road to Ensenada*

Horse's Neck

Serves 1

This is a classic cocktail, and we always say, "If it ain't broke, don't fix it." Many a young Southerner has ordered a "7 and 7," which is merely a weak imitation of this drink. (A Horse's Neck actually started out as an "unleaded beverage," until someone had the inspired idea of adding whiskey to it.) Classic cocktail names are sometimes difficult to interpret, but we think the name of this one may have something to do with the "whinny" that a whiff of potent ginger ale will give the unsuspecting quaffer.

> **1 fresh lemon**
> **2 ounces whiskey**
> **Dash of Angostura bitters**
> **4 ounces ginger ale**

With a channel knife or, if that's not available, a vegetable peeler, remove a spiral of lemon peel: start at the base and peel 'round and 'round so that you get a long piece of peel that spirals like a yellow slinky. Place the lemon peel spiral into a highball glass so that one end hooks over the rim of the glass and half-fill the glass with ice. Pour in the whiskey and bitters, and top with the ginger ale. Serve at breakneck speed.

RECOMMENDED LISTENING
"Ballad of a Runaway Horse,"
by Emmylou Harris,
from *Cowgirl's Prayer*

Goldminer's Cocktail

Serves 1

Of the two liqueurs containing gold, Goldschlager hails from Switzerland, though it's hard to believe that the Swiss, who are usually so conservative about money, came up with the idea of putting flakes of real gold into a liqueur. Goldschlager has proven amazingly popular with today's college students, by whom it is usually consumed as an ice-cold shot. The other liqueur is the much more refined Goldwasser, which comes from Gdansk in Poland (formerly called Danzig, when it was German—thus the correct name, Danziger Goldwasser). If you are a rabid fan of cinnamon, be our guests, but this concoction is much more genteel. The fluttering of the golden flakes will catch the light, and you may almost imagine discovering a priceless gold nugget at the bottom of your glass. If you have several of these, you may not need to find a nugget to find true happiness.

> **2 ounces dry gin**
> **1 ounce dry vermouth**
> **¹/₂ ounce Goldschlager**

Chill a small cocktail glass. In a cocktail shaker half-filled with ice, combine the gin and the vermouth. Shake hard and fast, then immediately strain into the chilled glass. Carefully "float" the Goldschlager on the top of the cocktail (see page 7), and serve before anyone cashes it in.

RECOMMENDED LISTENING
"A Poor Man's Roses (Or a Rich Man's Gold),"
by Patsy Cline,
from *Golden Classics*

Sonora Sangria

Serves 1

Virtually the Spanish national drink, a "Sangria" usually contains brandy and lots of fruit, though it is sometimes served without the brandy. Don't confuse it with a "Sangrita," which is a very different animal indeed. A sangrita is a non-alcoholic chaser for shots of tequila that's made from tomato, citrus juices, and green Tabasco. This hybrid version of the sangria crosses Latin cultural lines by combining Mexico's tequila with the Spanish Sangria tradition.

> 1 ounce tequila
> 1 ounce Triple Sec
> 3 ounces fruity red wine
> 2 ounces Reata Sweet 'n' Sour Mix (page 128)
> Splash of club soda
> Wedge of lime, for garnish
> Wedge of orange, for garnish

In a cocktail shaker half-filled with ice, combine the tequila, Triple Sec, red wine, and sweet-and-sour mix. Shake well, then immediately strain into a highball glass over ice. Add a splash of club soda, garnish with the lime and orange wedges, and serve.

RECOMMENDED LISTENING
"Spanish Two-Step,"
by Adolf Hofner,
from *Adolf Hofner's South Texas Swing*

Rusted Spur

Serves 1

The first giveaway for a drugstore cowboy is usually his shiny new spurs. Remember getting a new pair of white tennis shoes and rushing out into the dirt to scuff them up so your friends wouldn't think you were a sissy? Well, shiny spurs are worse.

> ³/₄ **ounce gold tequila**
> ³/₄ **ounce Absolut Citron vodka**
> ¹/₄ **ounce cinnamon schnapps**
> **Pinch of ground cinnamon**

In a cocktail shaker one-quarter filled with ice, combine the tequila, vodka, and schnapps. Shake hard and fast, then immediately strain into a standard shot glass. Sprinkle just a hint of cinnamon over the top and serve at once.

RECOMMENDED LISTENING
"Lone Star Rattlesnake Bar,"
by Clyde Edgerton,
from *Walking Across Egypt*

"The sun came out for our walk to the cabin, and when we got there I made Boone lunch and a couple of drinks. I mixed the Tang and the water separately from the rum so the drinks would taste real."
—from *Cowboys Are My Weakness,*
by Pam Houston.

© 1992 by Pam Houston. Reprinted by permission of W.W. Norton & Company, Inc.

5

QUENCHERS FROM THE GARDEN

ruity drinks may not seem like concoctions cowboys would choose. But today, cowboy is really just a state of mind, and when it's hot outside, you'll be happy to stir up one of these whimsical concoctions and find the nearest patch of shade. Many of these may remind you of the kind of refreshments we all used to order at the soda shop, but rest assured they've been well updated for adult tastes. Fruit seems to be a natural companion for strong spirits (limes and rum have been together since the British discovered that limes cured scurvy and started including them with the sailor's daily rum ration). Almost all cocktails are a combination of three basic flavors: strong (the spirits), sweet, and sour. After you try a drink once, feel free to mess around with the proportions if you like a sweeter or stronger flavor, or prefer more of a sour bite.

Just as time waits for no man, a cocktail waits for no man (or woman). If it's hot it should be served hot; if cold it must be served cold—either way, it's got to be served immediately. There's nothing more inviting than a freshly poured cocktail, with the shards of ice swirling around atop the smoky, frosted glass. Imagine the same cocktail ten minutes later, lonely and abandoned on the bar with no one to appreciate the passing of its prime. So make sure you've got everything on hand—including those who'll be drinking—before you starting mixing.

Sour Beer Punch

Serves 4

*A nice, gentle concoction for lunch under
an oak tree, while you munch on
Molasses-Glazed Chicken Wings (page
112) from the picnic basket and survey
your domain (whether it's your very own
ranch or the local park).*

3 lemons
1 cup sugar
1 cup water
$^1/_2$ cup chilled grapefruit juice
1 can light beer
Lemon slices, for garnish
Maraschino cherries, for garnish

Using a vegetable peeler, remove the zest from lemons, leaving behind
the white pith, and set aside (reserve the peeled lemons). In a
saucepan over high heat, combine the sugar and water and bring to a
boil, stirring until the sugar has dissolved. Add the lemon zest and
remove from the heat. Cover and let stand for 10 minutes. Remove and
discard the lemon zest from the mixture and let it cool to room temperature.

Juice the peeled lemons. Add the lemon juice and grapefruit juice
to the sugar mixture. Pour into a large serving pitcher and chill for at
least 2 hours. Just before serving, stir in the beer. Serve in glass mugs,
garnished with the lemon slices and cherries.

RECOMMENDED LISTENING
"Rollin' in My Sweet Baby's Arms,"
by George Jones,
from *Life Turned Her That Way*

Texas Lemonade

Serves 1

Sometimes it seems like a Texan's blood might run lemonade, we drink so much of it. But we'd never want to leave out our friends south of the border, so we've generously included tequila in this quenching cocktail. It's a true diplomatic gesture!

> **Wedge of fresh lemon, for frosting the glass**
> **Granulated sugar, for frosting the glass**
> **1¹/₂ ounces Herradura White Tequila**
> **1 ounce freshly squeezed lemon juice**
> **2 tablespoons superfine sugar**
> **2 slices Candied Limes (page 130), for garnish**

Moisten the rim of a mason jar or large tumbler with a lemon wedge. Dip the rim of the glass into a plate of granulated sugar to frost the rim, then fill the glass with ice. In a bar tumbler, combine the tequila, lemon juice, and superfine sugar. Stir until the sugar is completely dissolved. Strain into the prepared glass, garnish with the candied limes, and serve.

RECOMMENDED LISTENING
"Just Fine,"
by Pat Green,
from *Live at Billy Bob's Texas*

ANONYMOUS COWBOY QUOTE:

"Never drink unless you're alone or with somebody."

Afternoon Tea

Serves 6

Iced tea is right up there with lemonade as the non-alcoholic drink of choice throughout Texas and much of the South (we'd never mix the two together, like they do out in Hollywood). Looking for a way to spice up our afternoon tea, we came up with the perfect pairing of spiced rum and iced tea. Call all the ladies, shady and otherwise, and break out the cucumber sandwiches! Best enjoyed on a wide veranda.

> **2 quarts brewed tea, chilled**
> **8 ounces light spiced rum, such as Captain Morgan's Silver**
> **6 thin slices of lemon, for garnish**
> **6 sprigs of mint, for garnish**

Chill a large pitcher (about 10-cup capacity) and six highball or other tall glasses. Fill the pitcher halfway with ice, and stir the tea and the rum together in it. Serve over ice in the prepared glasses, garnished with the lemon slices and mint.

RECOMMENDED LISTENING
"That Ol' Wind,"
by Garth Brooks,
from *Fresh Horses*

Sittin' on the Porch

Serves 1

Southern Comfort is often referred to as "sippin' whiskey," because it goes down so smooth and silky. It's actually bourbon, and when paired with peach and cranberry, it makes a mood-altering, porch-sittin', sweet and rosy drink for the ladies and the cowboys, long as they swear to wipe their boots before they come up on the porch. Relax, set your sights on the horizon, and breathe it all in.

1^1/$_2$ ounces Southern Comfort
1 ounce peach schnapps
1 ounce cranberry juice
Wedge of lime, for garnish

Fill a Texas jigger or an old-fashioned glass with ice. Add the Southern Comfort, schnapps, and cranberry juice and stir to mix. Squeeze the lime into the glass, drop it in, and serve at once.

RECOMMENDED LISTENING
"Come a Little Bit Closer,"
by Jay & The Americans,
from *Come a Little Bit Closer*

Cherry-Vanilla Limeade

Serves 1

In the small towns of Texas circa 1950, the soda pops at the drugstore were what most kids lived for. Dropping in for a shot of syrupy-sweet soda was a chance to see friends, indulge a sweet tooth, and pick up the latest movie magazines (not to mention swooning over James Dean, Liz Taylor, and Rock Hudson). This is a soda-stand special with a grown-up twist.

Note: *Vanilla beans are expensive, but luckily they can be used over and over again before they lose their intense, exotic perfume. Just be sure to rinse and let dry completely before storing in a zip-top bag, otherwise the bean may develop a nasty case of mildew.*

> **2 ounces Stoli Vanil vodka**
> **1 ounce Grenadine**
> **Juice of 1 lime**
> **Splash of Sprite**
> **1 vanilla bean, for garnish**

Half-fill a highball or other tall glass with ice. Add the vodka, Grenadine, and lime juice. Stir to mix and top with a generous splash of Sprite. Place the vanilla bean in the drink and serve.

RECOMMENDED LISTENING
"Grapefruit, Juicy Fruit,"
by Jimmy Buffett,
from *Songs You Know by Heart*

Peach-Melon Cooler

Serves 1

This is a perfect drink for strolling—strolling in your garden, strolling down to the chicken coop, or strolling by the pool on a hot Sunday afternoon. The Sprite adds a welcome fizzy lift to the cocktail. And if you'd like a tamer version, just make the drink in a tall glass and increase the Sprite.

> 2 ounces Reata Sweet 'n' Sour Mix (page 128)
> 1 ounce Midori Melon liqueur
> 1 ounce peach schnapps
> Splash of Sprite
> Sprig of fresh mint, for garnish

Fill a Texas jigger or an old-fashioned glass halfway with ice. Add the sweet-and-sour mix, Midori, and schnapps. Stir to blend thoroughly. Top with a splash of Sprite, garnish with the mint, and serve.

RECOMMENDED LISTENING
"Cowboy Boots and Bathin' Suits,"
by Jerry Jeff Walker,
from *Cowboy Boots and Bathin' Suits*

Pumpkin Pie

Serves 1

Close your eyes and think of Thanksgiving! Honestly, this concoction tastes exactly like a wedge of Grandma's best. To "layer" a drink, pour each individual liquor slowly over the back of an inverted teaspoon held about a half inch above the surface of the drink. Layer the liquors in the order given and be careful not to disturb the glass, or the lovely striped effect will be lost. (Invented by the bartender at Reata, Alpine, in a moment of pure inspiration—or maybe he missed his Ma.)

> ³/₄ **ounce Kahlua**
> ¹/₄ **ounce cinnamon schnapps**
> ¹/₂ **ounce Bailey's Irish Cream**
> ¹/₄ **ounce Bacardi 151 Rum**
> **Pinch of ground nutmeg**
> **Pinch of ground cloves**

In a 2-ounce shot glass, carefully layer the Kahlua, the cinnamon schnapps, and then the Bailey's. Finally, "float" with the Bacardi 151 (see page 7). Carefully light the shot with a long match and sprinkle the spices over the flame. Blow out the flame and drink quickly.

RECOMMENDED LISTENING
"Waltz Across Texas,"
by Waylon Jennings,
from *Ladies Love Outlaws*

Texas Tea

Serves 1

Long Island Iced Tea was popular in the seventies, and for very good reason—it is a delicious drink. Texas introduces its own version with this contender, made extra-special by the addition of Tito's Texas vodka and that far-off relative of prune juice: Dr Pepper (invented in Texas, of course!).

$^1/_2$ **ounce tequila**
$^1/_2$ **ounce Triple Sec**
$^1/_2$ **ounce white rum**
$^1/_2$ **ounce Tito's Texas vodka**
Splash of Sprite
Splash of Dr Pepper
2 aspirin, any brand

Fill a highball glass halfway with ice. In a shaker half-filled with ice, combine the tequila, Triple Sec, rum, and vodka. Shake hard and fast, then immediately strain into the prepared glass. Top with the Sprite and Dr Pepper. Stir to mix, and serve with the aspirin on the side.

RECOMMENDED LISTENING
"Sunset on the Sage,"
by Commander Cody,
from *Live from Deep in the Heart of Texas*

Reata's "Famous" Bloody Mary

Serves 8

It seems like everybody and every bar has a "best" version of the Bloody Mary, a drink that has kept its huge popularity untarnished for generations. What makes the Reata version great is the extensive and laborious testing that has gone into making the "Mary Mix" just right. Of course, one man's perfection might be another man's mouth-burner—so adjust and tinker with the heat and strength of this concoction till it fits you and your loved ones like a worn-out shoe.

4 crisp ribs of celery, halved lengthwise
5 cups Reata's Famous Blood Mary Mix
   (page 128)
16 ounces vodka

Place the celery in a bowl of ice water and let stand, refrigerated, for 30 minutes. Half-fill 8 double old-fashioned glasses with ice. Pour 5 ounces (²/₃ cup) bloody mary mix into each glass and top with 2 ounces of vodka. Stir well and garnish with the celery sticks.

RECOMMENDED LISTENING
"I'll Never Get out of This World Alive,"
by Hank Williams Sr.,
from *40 Greatest Hits*

Texas Applesauce

Serves 2

Texan Grant Kernan went up to New Hampshire and invented this frothy concoction to add a little kick to the local favorite "hard" cider (it took a Texan to figure it out!). It looks like a glass full of applesauce and tastes dee-licious.

3 ounces whiskey
12 ounces Woodchuck Hard Cider
Wedges of fresh apple, for garnish

Chill a double old-fashioned glass. In a blender, combine the whiskey, cider, and two scoops of crushed ice. Blend until smooth and pour into the prepared glass. Garnish the edge of the glass with the apple wedge and serve immediately.

RECOMMENDED LISTENING
"Ride 'Em, Cowboy,"
by Juice Newton,
from *Trouble with Angels*

> "Hospitality in the prairie country is not limited. Even if your enemy passes your way, you must feed him before you shoot him."
>
> —O. Henry

Red Rooster

Serves 1

This is a traditional Tex-Mex hangover cure, and there's no doubt it's a real good wake-up call. We prescribe this if you mistakenly consumed too many Cowboy Cocktails the night before. A word from the liquid wise: let just one of these last for a good long while before moving on to a more serious picker-upper, and throw in the all-time, hands-down answer to a mean hangover—vigorous exercise (walking to the mailbox doesn't count, by the way).

> **3 ounces Reata's Famous Bloody Mary Mix (page 128)**
> **1 bottle Lone Star beer**
> **1 Pickled Jalapeño Pepper (page 130), for garnish**

Chill a large beer mug. Combine the bloody mary mix and beer in the mug, garnish with the jalapeño, and serve immediately.

RECOMMENDED LISTENING
"The Bottle,"
by Pat Green,
from *Dancehall Dreamer*

Cowboy Roy

Serves 4

Instead of a Shirley Temple, Texas youngsters were served a Roy Rogers while the adults quaffed their cocktails (it is basically the same drink). When you and your friends feel like being kids, consider this adult version of a Roy Rogers.

- **6 ounces vodka**
- **2 ounces grenadine**
- **24 ounces fresh or best-quality bottled orange juice**
- **1 can ginger ale**
- **4 lime wedges, for garnish**

Half-fill four Texas jiggers or old-fashioned glasses with ice. In a large pitcher, combine the vodka, grenadine, orange juice, and ginger ale. Stir together to mix and pour into the prepared glasses. Garnish each glass with a lime wedge and serve.

RECOMMENDED LISTENING
"All Grown Up,"
by Jimmie Dale Gilmore,
from *Fair & Square*

LITTLE-KNOWN FACT:

Many people think Texas is one big, treeless wasteland. Not so. Texas sports one hundred fifty different varieties of trees and has about twenty-three million forested acres. In 1907, Texas ranked third in the country in lumber production—these days it's more like sixth or eighth. Certainly not a barren wasteland.

6

SOOTHING SUNDOWNERS

You don't have to really be a cowboy to feel like one. Feeling like a cowboy might mean acting a little bit tough and walking with a slight bow-legged swagger when you step into your favorite bar, or it might mean tipping your hat at the next prime cowboy or cowgirl that crosses your path. But one thing all true cowboys certainly feel at the end of the day is worn out. Real cowboys live a hard, unforgiving life, and the sunset seems like a blessing from heaven. They say that the sunsets in West Texas come about as close to heaven as you can get, and we're inclined to agree.

When someone once asked Jimmy Buffett where "Margaritaville" was, he answered, "It's wherever you want it to be." And sundown is a little like that, too. You can imagine yourself just about anywhere as you gaze into the golden light that creeps across the land when the sun gets low on the horizon. You might be sitting on the fence with a few cronies, crowing about all the barbed wire you strung today, or you might be on the balcony of a high-rise watching the sun set above the city's smoke and dust. Either way, it's a state of mind that lets you put the day to bed and imagine that tomorrow won't be nearly as bad. The perfect drink for such an occasion is, of course, a "sundowner."

Montana Cowboy

Serves 2

Up in Big Sky country there's always something that needs doing, whether it's mending fences or watering the lawn. That is, until the sun starts to set and that big sky turns all the shades of indigo, with those wispy little straggler clouds stretched out along the horizon. For those pensive moments, try this smooth and spicy libation.

4 ounces Canadian whiskey
2 ounces heavy cream
Pinch of ground nutmeg

Chill a large cocktail glass. In a shaker half-filled with ice, combine the whiskey and cream. Shake hard and fast, then immediately strain into the prepared glass. Garnish with the nutmeg and serve in a big way.

RECOMMENDED LISTENING
"Girl from the North Country,"
by Johnny Cash with Bob Dylan,
from *The Man in Black*

COWBOY VOCABULARY:

Dogies = cows and calves

Marfa Light

Serves 1

Marfa is a little town about thirty miles from Alpine, where the original Reata is located. It's become famous for its mysterious lights, so we concocted this cocktail in its honor—and it's often helped us see our own version of the Marfa lights.

> **2 ounces Midori Melon Liqueur**
> **1 ounce bourbon**
> **Splash of Blue Curaçao**
> **1 ounce Reata Sweet 'n' Sour Mix (page 128)**

In a bar tumbler filled halfway with ice, combine the Midori, bourbon, Curaçao, and sweet-and-sour mix. Stir well and strain into a chilled cocktail glass. Serve before the lights go out.

RECOMMENDED LISTENING
"The Light,"
by Emmylou Harris,
from *Cowgirl's Prayer*

El Postre

Serves 1

El postre *means dessert in Spanish, and the butterscotch schnapps here certainly makes this sweet cocktail qualify. Besides that, this drink is much easier to make than peach cobbler when you feel a hankering for something sweet after supper.*

>   1$^1/_2$ ounces tequila
>   1 ounce Bailey's Irish Cream
> $^1/_2$ ounce butterscotch schnapps
>   Half-and-half to taste

Fill a Texas jigger or an old-fashioned glass halfway with ice. In a bar tumbler half-filled with ice, combine the tequila, Bailey's, and schnapps. Stir well and strain into the prepared glass. Top with a little half-and-half and gobble it up.

RECOMMENDED LISTENING
"Cancion del Mariachi,"
by Los Lobos,
from the *Desperado* soundtrack

Red River Punch

Serves 4

This is a refined little champagne punch that makes a nice start to an outdoor party—if you're in Texas, that'd be steak on the grill, of course. In the early days, steaks were cut "on the hoof" and cooked well done or not at all. Now, steaks are aged and often cooked to a gorgeous blood-red medium rare—but then again, today's cattle are mighty different now from those early longhorns. Tough? Cowboy vocabulary gives us this hint: "Tough as a trail-drive steak." (Tuaca is an Italian liqueur flavored with citrus and herbs. It's a pale honey color and tastes a little bit like butterscotch.)

> 8 ounces Reata Sweet 'n' Sour Mix (page 128)
> 4 ounces Chambord liqueur
> 4 ounces Tuaca Citrus Liqueur
> 1 bottle sparkling wine
> Edible flowers, such as violas or nasturtiums, for garnish

Half-fill a large pitcher with ice. Add the sweet-and-sour mix, Chambord, Tuaca, and sparkling wine and stir to mix. Serve in punch cups, garnished with the edible flowers. Serve before the bubbles tickle your nose.

RECOMMENDED LISTENING
"Miles and Miles of Texas,"
by Asleep at the Wheel,
from *Best of Asleep at the Wheel*

Purple Jesus

Serves 1

We've always felt that the world needed a purple drink, and not just because it gives us the chance to say, "I don't care if it rains or freezes, as long as I've got my Purple Jesus. "

1¹/₂ ounces Tito's Texas vodka
3 ounces Welch's grape juice
2 ounces ginger ale, or to taste
Red grapes, for garnish

In a highball glass half-filled with ice, combine the vodka, grape juice, and ginger ale. Stir to mix and garnish with the grapes. Serve for a religious experience.

RECOMMENDED LISTENING
"Honky Tonk Heroes,"
by Waylon Jennings,
from *Honky Tonk Heroes*

Long Day on the Trail

Serves 1

Every hard-drivin' man or woman deserves a fine end to a tough day. After all, don't you deserve it? (Anyone says you don't, and you can threaten a serious pummeling.)

2 ounces premium Cognac (the best you can afford)
1 premium cigar

Pour the Cognac into a small snifter glass. Cut off the cigar tip and soak the cigar in the Cognac for several seconds. Light the cigar in your preferred manner. Sip on the Cognac while periodically dipping the cigar as you smoke. Relax and kick your boots off—this day, at least, is over.

RECOMMENDED LISTENING
"Closing Time,"
by Radney Foster,
from *Del Rio TX 1959*

"My limbs are weary and my seat is
    all sore,
Lay down, dogies, like you laid down
    before.
Lay down, little dogies, lay down"
    —from the "Night Herding Song,"
        by Harry Stephens, 1909

Last Dance

Serves 1

When you live in Texas, you aren't likely to set out in the evening for the theater or the opera. More likely, it'll be a football game or a dance. Before the cowfolks became citified, Texans had to make their own entertainment—and dancing was always the most popular. The last dance was a bittersweet moment, when the fun of the evening was winding down. Cowhands had to head back to their camps, and gals had to go home with mom and pop. Bittersweet, just like the final cocktail in this book.

> 1^1/$_2$ ounces tequila
> 1 ounce Crème de Cacao
> 1^1/$_2$ ounces heavy cream
> Dash of grenadine
> Pinch of ground cinnamon

In a shaker half-filled with ice, combine the tequila, Crème de Cacao, cream, and grenadine. Shake to a two-step rhythm, then strain into an old-fashioned glass. Serve before the guests start to yawn.

RECOMMENDED LISTENING
"It Shall Be a Midnight Music,"
by Jerry Jeff Walker,
from *A Man Must Carry On, Vol. 2*

T. R. Fehrenbach observed in his book *Lone Star: A History of Texas and the Texans,* that "empiricism" was a key feature of the early Texan's way of thinking. The "empirical mind" sees things only in terms of cause and effect—i.e. not how things *might* be, but how they are *right here* (ra-cheer) and *right now*. Taking the concept even further, you might say that all knowledge must result from experience, none from theory (in other words, if you haven't seen a man walk on the moon with your own two eyes, then it didn't happen). This stubborn mindset was probably a side-effect of trying to create a civilization in a harsh, unforgiving environment. So, the next time you meet a stubborn Texan, just agree with him or her, then smile privately to yourself and blame empirical thinking.

7

UNLEADED BEVERAGES

Seven

here are many times when a non-alcoholic drink is the libation of choice, and it's not just for the underaged (though they deserve to have their fun, too). You may be recovering from too many Cowboy Cocktails the night before, you may be "on the wagon," as our parents' generation used to say, or you may be picnicking before a big baseball game or a rodeo. Whether you're a permanent "teetotaller" or just a temporary one, you'll need some flavorful quenchers for the old repertoire.

It must be mentioned that for much of this century, many counties in Texas were "dry" (in other words, no alcohol could be sold within the county lines). In some places, 3.2 beer was legal, but it could never be sold cold. This resulted in several generations of Texans growing up with a fond affection for warm, weak beer. There are still quite a few dry counties in the South (eighty in Texas alone). Dry county or not, these are some great non-alcoholic drink choices that will quench your thirst and soothe your spirit.

Sarsaparilla Sno-Cone

Serves 2

Sarsaparilla was a crucial ingredient in drugstore shakes in the early part of the century, and it was made from the oils of the European birch tree and sassafras, a variety of laurel. Easterners may be lucky enough to find birch beer, and sarsaparilla is still available in some parts of the South. It's a unique and addictive flavor, but root beer comes close enough to satisfy, too.

> **2 cups ice cubes**
> **2 cups root beer or sarsaparilla**
> **1 cup heavy cream**

In a blender, combine the ice, root beer, and cream. Blend until smooth and slushy and serve in highball glasses.

"Pop, pop, pop! Bom, bom, bom! throughout the day. No time for memorandums now. Go ahead. Liberty and Independence forever!"
—last entry in Davy Crockett's journal, The Alamo, March 5, 1836
(Crockett went to Texas in a huff after losing a congressional election in Tennessee and died for the independence of his adopted land).

Mango Sno-Cone

Serves 2

Mango is a sweet, rich fruit that will defy those who have not been shown how to free the pesky pit from the fibrous inner fruit. Remember two things: (1) the pit is flat and oval in shape—once you find out (by probing with a sharp knife) which way the flat part is facing, it's easy to carve it out; and (2) mango fruit is widely available in glass jars, sans pit.

> $^1/_2$ **fresh mango, peeled, pit removed, and chopped**
> **2 cups pineapple juice**
> $^1/_2$ **cup coconut cream**
> **1 cup ice cubes**
> **2 mint sprigs, for garnish**

In a blender, purée the mango, pineapple juice, coconut cream, and ice until smooth and slushy. Pour into large cocktail glasses and garnish with mint sprigs.

When adults are consuming cocktails of the stronger variety, try whipping up a Dr Pepper Moo or a Mango Sno-Cone for the little ones instead of palming them off with the usual sodas—it'll make them feel more a part of the festivities.

Virgin Cherry-Vanilla Limeade

Serves 2

Non-alcoholic fruit syrups are widely available at gourmet shops and good markets. Their flavors range from lemon to raspberry to vanilla, and often everything in between. They provide a quick and easy way to add flavor to drinks of all descriptions.

> 2 cups club soda
> Juice of 3 limes (about 3 $^1/_2$ ounces)
> 2 tablespoons vanilla syrup (such as Torani)
> Splash of grenadine

Fill 2 large cocktail glasses with crushed ice. Divide the soda, lime juice, vanilla, and grenadine equally among the glasses. Stir well and serve at once.

Strawberry-Lemonade Fizz

Serves 6 to 8

This drink uses frozen strawberries instead of ice to provide the slush content that is so crucial in summer beverages, especially in very hot climates. This is a gorgeous cocktail that will make even designated drivers feel greatly loved.

> **2 cups frozen strawberries**
> **1 cup freshly squeezed lemon juice**
> **$1/2$ cup sugar, or to taste**
> **3 cups 7-Up or Sprite**
> **Slices of lime, for garnish**
> **Fresh strawberries, for garnish**

Sugar-frost the rims of 6 or 8 highball glasses (see page 7), and half-fill them with ice. In a blender, combine the strawberries, lemon juice, and sugar. Purée the mixture until smooth and slushy. Strain into a large pitcher and add the 7-Up. Mix well, garnish with the lime and strawberries, and serve in the prepared glasses.

Virgin La Paloma

Serves 2

The La Paloma, virtually the national drink of Guadalajara, combines tequila, lemon juice, and Squirt (a vastly under-appreciated carbonated grapefruit beverage that also mixes well with rum). This variation brings all the excitement without the punch.

> **2 cups Squirt**
> **Juice of 3 limes (about 3^1/$_2$ ounces)**
> **4 tablespoons granulated sugar**

Sugar-frost the rims of two large cocktail glasses (see page 7), and fill them with crushed or cracked ice. In a cocktail shaker half-filled with ice, combine the Squirt, lime juice, and sugar. Shake hard and fast, then immediately pour into the prepared glasses and serve.

Dr Pepper Moo

Serves 2

Mmmm, mmmm good. Dr Pepper was born in Texas in 1885, a cow state if there ever was one. Here, the pride of prune juice everywhere meets the cattle-raising tradition in a sweet, satisfying sundowner.

2 cups Dr Pepper
$^1/_2$ cup half-and-half or heavy cream

Fill two large old-fashioned glasses with ice. Pour the Dr Pepper over the ice and wait a moment for the foam to settle. Drizzle the half-and-half over the tops of the drinks, and stir gently to swirl the cream around just slightly.

Melon-Up

Serves 2 to 4

Liquados are hugely popular juice drinks south of the border that combine fruit, ice, and milk. Our variation on the liquado swears off milk and goes up, and up, and away!

> $^1/_2$ **cantaloupe, peeled, seeded, and diced**
> **2 cups bottled spring water or your favorite tap water**
> $^1/_4$ **cup granulated sugar**
> **2 cups 7-Up**
> **Splash of grenadine**
> **Balls of cantaloupe, for garnish**
> **Balls of honeydew, for garnish**

In a blender, combine the cantaloupe, water, and sugar and purée until smooth. Strain through a fine strainer into a large pitcher. Stir in the 7-Up and grenadine, garnish with the melon balls, and serve in tall glasses.

"Haying was a delightful season for us, for the scythes of the men occasionally tossed up clusters of beautiful strawberries, which we joyfully gathered. I remember with especial pleasure the delicious shortcakes which my mother made of the wild fruit which we picked in the warm odorous grass along the edge of the meadow. Harvest time also brought a pleasing excitement (something unwonted, something like entertaining visitors) which compensated for the extra work demanded of us. The neighbors usually came in to help and life was a feast."

—Hamlin Garland, who lived in the
Dakota territories in the 1880s,
from *A Son of the Middle Border*

8

TASTY VITTLES

Eight

or the original cowboys out on the range, fine dining was not an option. They ate in shifts, because someone always had to be watching the cattle, and the fare was not glorious. However, it was the one thing cowboys could look forward to in their hard, dusty days. Camp cooks were often older cowboys whose bones were just too tired to go on being cowboys. If they were good at making chuck, they'd get a good reputation, and the ranch would have no trouble recruiting hands for the season. If a cook didn't do so well, he'd be the butt of ridicule and endless jokes.

It couldn't have been an easy job. The cook had to travel ahead of the herd so he could set up camp and start the fire. The diet was made up of beans, bread, and meat, and the cowboys worked hard so they needed plenty of it. The beans had to cook for hours, so the cook would start them first, then start the biscuits and pies in a heavy Dutch oven, and finally make the strong, bitter, and grainy coffee that the cowhands loved so well. Of course there was no refrigeration, so a cow would be killed on the trail, left to cool overnight, and butchered the next day (trouble-making steers were often culled in this way). Since this meat was invariably about as tough as old boots, it needed long cooking. Chili became a useful recipe for softening the tough meat while at the same time disguising its possibly "off" flavor with strong, hot spices. Steaks, when they were consumed, were always cooked to beyond the well-done stage (traveling Texans in movies from the 50s often shouted to a beleaguered city chef, "Take this steak back in the kitchen and *burn it!*").

There was no yeast available, so a piece of dough was saved from the previous day's bread and used to "start" the next day's loaves (this was the origin of sourdough bread). Woe to the cookie who forgot to save out a piece of dough, or let the natural yeasts in it die—there'd be no bread until he could beg, borrow, or steal a piece of dough from another chuck wagon! When the meal had been consumed, the cook had to wash all the dishes (or scrub them with sand, if water wasn't available, which was often the case), sew on any stray buttons and mend any split seams, then dole out medical supplies from his rudimentary first-aid kit. He was also responsible for repairing broken wheels and struts on the chuck wagon itself. It's not hard to imagine how camp cooks on the range got the reputation for being mean and crusty, bad-tempered old souls (hence the saying, "Cussin' a camp cook is as risky as brandin' a mule's tail.").

Today, chuck wagons are towed behind gleaming crew-cabs and cooks dole out far more sophisticated fare, but it's still based on the original cowboy diet of beans, bread, and meat. The Mexican influence so pervasive in Texas and cowboy culture continues to add flavor and excitement to today's cowboy cuisine, just as it has since the first camp cook discovered that adding powdered chiles to a boring beef stew turned it into some mighty tasty vittles.

Albondigas

Yield: 60 meatballs

Albondigas are meatballs from south of the border. What a great, easy, and awe-some party food—Grady once ate twenty-two of these at the CF Ranch Fourth of July party! And for a little variety, try substituting ground lamb, pork, or even chicken. You'll love them, we guarantee it.

2 pounds ground chuck, 20 percent fat content

3 eggs, beaten

1 large yellow onion, diced

1 large red bell pepper, stemmed, seeded, and diced

3 jalapeño peppers, stemmed, and diced

3 tablespoons Worcestershire sauce

4 large cloves garlic, minced

$^1/_2$ cup ketchup

2 teaspoons granulated sugar

$1^1/_2$ teaspoons kosher salt, or to taste

Preheat the oven to 425°F. In a large mixing bowl, combine all the ingredients and mix thoroughly by hand. Divide the mixture into 1-ounce balls (large walnut sized), rolling them between the palms of your hands until firm and round. Place the albondigas on a lightly oiled baking sheet and bake for about 15 minutes, or until firm, bubbling, and golden on the bottoms. Serve on a napkin-lined plate.

Pan Del Campos

Yield: 9 servings

Pan Del Campo means "camp bread" along the Texas-Mexico border. We like to think of it as "cowboy pizza." Try these variations, or be creative and make up your own. The crusts can be stored indefinitely and used like crackers with dips and spreads.

1 pound (about 20 slices) bacon
1 package refrigerated biscuit dough
$^1/_2$ cup flour, for dusting
$^1/_2$ cup Cilantro-Pecan Mash (page 121)
$^1/_2$ pound fresh field greens
2 large, ripe tomatoes, sliced into thin rounds
5 cups (1 pound) grated Monterey Jack cheese

Preheat the oven to 375°F. In a heavy skillet, cook the bacon until very crisp (cook in batches if necessary to prevent overcrowding). Drain on paper towels and set aside.

Remove the biscuit dough from the package and separate into 8 individual pieces. Sprinkle some flour on a clean, dry work surface, flour a rolling pin, and roll each of the dough pieces out to approximately 9-inch rounds. Don't be afraid to roll them out thin, because the thinner they are, the crisper, lighter, and better they'll be. Carefully transfer them to baking sheets and bake for about 10 minutes, until bread is golden brown and crisp, checking occasionally to be sure they don't burn. Remove the crusts from the oven

Increase the oven to 400°F. Spread each crust with some of the cilantro mash. Scatter the field greens and tomatoes on each "pizza," and then sprinkle each one generously with crumbled bacon and grated cheese. Return to the oven for two or three more minutes to melt the cheese and serve at once.

pan del

campos

Pork Picadillo Rolls

Yield: 16 rolls

These tasty little critters are a breeze to throw together for some quick party food. And, you can easily vary the fillings depending on taste and what's on hand in the kitchen. We often substitute chicken, beef, shrimp, or an all-time favorite, cabrito (baby goat).

> **2 packages refrigerated biscuit dough**
> **$^1/_4$ cup flour, for dusting**
> **1 cup grated Monterey Jack cheese**
> **$1^1/_2$ cups Pork Picadillo (recipe below)**
> **Olive oil for brushing**
> **2 tablespoons kosher salt**

Pork Picadillo

Yield: $1^1/_2$ cups

> **2 tablespoons vegetable oil**
> **1 pound ground pork**
> **2 cloves garlic, minced**
> **$^1/_2$ yellow onion, chopped**
> **1 jalapeño pepper, stemmed, seeded, and chopped**
> **1 medium tomato, seeded and chopped**
> **2 tablespoons chile powder**
> **Juice of $^1/_2$ lime**
> **2 tablespoons chopped fresh cilantro**
> **$^3/_4$ teaspoon kosher salt, or to taste**

To prepare the filling, heat the oil in a large skillet over high heat. Add the garlic, onion, and jalapeño and sauté for about 2 minutes, or until the onions have begun to soften. Add the pork and cook for about 6 minutes more, or until the pork is golden. Add the tomato, chile powder, and lime juice and continue cooking for 6 or 7 minutes, until the mixture thickens slightly. Remove from the heat and add the cilantro and salt. Stir to combine and taste for seasoning. Set aside.

Preheat the oven to 375°F. Remove the biscuit dough from the package and separate into 8 individual pieces. Slice each piece in half horizontally to yield 16 thin biscuit rounds. Sprinkle some flour on a clean, dry work surface, flour a rolling pin, and roll out each biscuit to $1/4$-inch thickness.

To assemble the rolls, place about 1 heaping tablespoon of the filling in the middle of each round, mounding in the center and leaving a $3/8$-inch border. Sprinkle each one with some of the cheese, and then fold the round into a half-moon shape. Lightly press the edges together to seal. Sprinkle one large or two smaller baking sheets with flour. Place the rolls on the sheet(s), leaving about 2 inches between each one. Brush the top of each roll with a little olive oil and bake for 15 minutes, or until golden brown. Serve warm, with assorted condiments on the side, such as bottled or fresh salsa, ketchup, or hot sauce.

INDIGENOUS TEXAS CHOW, circa 1890 to 1935: Chili made with old, tough beef, lots of spices, and no beans (this is just as important now as it was then—the beans are served on the side, and don't you forget it).

INDIGENOUS TEXAS CHOW, circa 2000: Frito Pie (Get a bag of Fritos, which are made in Texas. Open the bag. Pour in chili. Add cheese and onions, if desired. Grab a spoon and dig in.)

Lone Star Shrimp Sandwich

Yield: 4 sandwiches

When Grady goes fishing on the Gulf Coast, his favorite form of nourishment is a shrimp sandwich. Shrimp prepared in this way also make fantastic appetizers—just serve with your favorite dippin' sauce. Be sure to have all of the elements of this delicious sandwich assembled before you start frying so that you can serve while the shrimp are still warm and crisp.

> **Vegetable oil for frying**
> **1 batch Lone Star Beer Batter (recipe follows)**
> **1 pound large shrimp, peeled and deveined**
> **8 slices sourdough bread, lightly toasted**
> **$1/_2$ cup mixed baby greens, romaine, or butter lettuce leaves**
> **1 ripe tomato, sliced into thin rounds**
> **Red Chile Mayo (page 120)**

In a heavy skillet over high heat, heat 2 inches of oil to 350°F (a drop of batter should sizzle when dropped in the oil). Dip each shrimp in the beer batter, then carefully slide them into the skillet so that the oil doesn't spatter. The shrimp will only take a few minutes to cook through depending on their size. They are done when the batter turns golden brown. Remove the shrimp with a slotted spoon and drain briefly on paper towels.

To assemble the sandwiches, spread the toasted bread slices with the mayo, and arrange tomato slices, lettuce, and shrimp on the bottom slice. Bon Appetit!

Lone Star Beer Batter

1 cup club soda
1 cup Lone Star or any good beer (drink the rest!)
1 tablespoon kosher salt
1 teaspoon red pepper flakes
1¹/₂ cups all-purpose flour

In a stainless steel or glass bowl, combine the soda, beer, salt, and pepper flakes. Start whisking and gradually whisk in the flour, blending thoroughly so there are no lumps. When the batter sticks to your finger, it's ready. If it seems thin, whisk in a little more flour (the batter should be thicker than heavy cream in consistency).

COWBOY VOCABULARY: *Hungry*

"I'd shore like to grease my chin with a two pound steak."

"My belly button is rubbing a blister on my backbone."

"I feel like a post hole that ain't been filled up."

"He shore was narrow at the equator."

"His tapeworm was hollerin' for fodder."

"He dug in like a wolf after guts."

CF Burgers

Yield: 6 burgers

Every Friday night, Grady and his partner Al used to host the Fun Friday Night Social Club at the Reata in Alpine. One night they served these burgers, named after Al's Texas ranch, to a bunch of actors and crew who were in town making a movie, and they were a huge hit. They've been on the menu ever since.

3 pounds ground chuck
$1/4$ cup blue cheese, such as Maytag
$1/4$ cup Onion Marmalade (page 124)
2 tablespoons Reata Grill Blend (page 122)
6 good-quality burger buns

Prepare and light the grill, and heat to medium-high, or preheat the oven to 375°F.

In a large mixing bowl, combine the ground chuck, blue cheese, onion marmalade, and grill blend. Blend thoroughly, using your hands. Divide and form into six 12-ounce patties, patting together loosely without compacting the meat too much. Arrange the patties on the grill and cook for 7 or 8 minutes on each side for medium-rare, or to your desired degree of doneness. If using the oven, bake for 25 minutes, or until done to your liking.

Serve with the onion marmalade or try out some of our extraordinary condiments, like Red Chile Mayo (page 120), Fruit Mustard (page 120), or Marinated Tomatoes (page 115), just for a change.

Dr Pepper Tacos

Yield: 8 tacos

Back before fancy meat tenderizers were available, folks used to marinate tougher meat in Coca-Cola because of its acidic content. We prefer Dr Pepper because it has more sugar. When you cook the meat, the sugar caramelizes, adding a great flavor. Besides, Dr Pepper was invented in Texas, as we may have mentioned.

> 1 (16-ounce) bottle of Dr Pepper
> 4 cloves garlic, peeled
> 2 cinnamon sticks
> 2 tablespoons Reata Grill Blend (page 122)
> 1^1/$_2$ pounds flank steak
> 8 large flour tortillas
> 8 corn tortillas

In a large bowl, combine the Dr Pepper, garlic cloves, and cinnamon sticks. Add the flank steak, cover with plastic wrap, and refrigerate for 12 hours.

Prepare and light the grill, and heat to medium-high. Remove the flank steak from the marinade and pat dry with paper towels. Season both sides with the grill blend. Grill the steak for 3 or 4 minutes on each side, or until done (never cook flank steak past the medium-rare stage or it will be very tough). Remove the steak from the grill and let rest for 4 or 5 minutes, loosely covered with foil. Cut the steak across the grain into 1-inch-wide slices. Serve hot with tortillas and your favorite condiments, such as Avocado Sour Cream or Pico de Gallo (page 117).

dr pepper

tacos

Lone Star-Battered Rib-Eye Strips

Yield: 4 servings

These delicioso little strips also make a perfect light meal served over fresh field greens with a spiced-up ranch dressing. Or, use as a filling for pita sandwiches. For maximum flavor power, serve as little appetizers. Your friends will love you.

> **2 cups peanut oil**
> **1 batch Lone Star Beer Batter (page 103)**
> **1 (16-ounce) rib-eye steak, cut into 1-inch strips across the grain**
> **Salt to taste**

In a heavy skillet over high heat, heat the oil to 375°F. Dredge the rib-eye strips in the batter, then carefully slide them into the skillet so that the oil doesn't spatter. They will only take a few minutes to cook and are done when the batter turns golden brown. Drain on paper towels, season to taste with salt, and serve hot.

VARIATION: Lone Star-Battered Chicken: Follow the recipe above but substitute two 8-ounce boneless, skinless chicken breasts cut into 1-inch strips. Be sure not to overcook.

Pitchfork Steak Fajitas

Yield: 8 fajitas

The "pitchfork" in the title refers to using an actual pitchfork to stab several steaks and hold them in a large vat of hot oil, instead of using tongs. This may be impractical in your home kitchen.

> 2 (16-ounce) rib-eye steaks
> 3 tablespoons Reata Grill Blend (page 122)
> 2 cups peanut oil
> 8 large flour or corn tortillas, warm
> $1/2$ pound shredded cabbage or lettuce
> Assorted condiments, such as Guacamole de Ojinaga (page 119) or
>   Pico de Gallo (page 117)
> 1 cup (4 ounces) grated Queso Cachiote or Monterey Jack cheese

Season both sides of the steaks with the grill blend and refrigerate, covered, for 2 to 3 hours.

In a large, deep skillet or Dutch oven over high heat, heat the oil to 375°F. Carefully slide the steaks into the hot oil using a meat fork or long, sturdy tongs. Cook for $3^1/2$ minutes per side, or until desired temperature. Remove the steaks from the skillet and set aside on a paper towel-lined platter to rest for 5 to 10 minutes, loosely covered with foil. Slice the steaks crosswise into 1-inch strips. Remember, the steaks will continue to cook for a few minutes after they've been removed from the skillet, so don't overcook them.

Assembling the fajitas is the fun part: have your guests each take a tortilla, fill it with some of the steak strips, and then pile on whatever else they like from the assortment you provide.

texas strip steak

nachos

Texas Strip Steak Nachos

Yield: 4 appetizer servings

If you happen to have any leftover pork asado on hand, substitute it for the steak in this recipe for another delicious variation.

1 (16-ounce) strip or rib-eye steak
2 tablespoons Reata Grill Blend (page 122)
5 corn tortillas, quartered
2 cups ($1/2$ pound) grated Monterey Jack cheese
3 jalapeño peppers, stemmed and thinly sliced crosswise
2 ripe avocados, peeled, seeded, and sliced, for garnish
$1/2$ cup sour cream, for garnish

Prepare and light the grill, and preheat it to medium-high. Season the steak with the grill blend. Grill for 3 to 4 minutes on each side, or until medium-rare. Set aside. While steak is resting, preheat the oven to 375°F.

Arrange the tortilla quarters on a baking sheet. Distribute the grated cheese evenly over the tortillas. Slice the steak on the diagonal into about 16 strips. Place the steak strips over the cheese-covered tortillas and sprinkle the jalapeños on top. Bake for 10 minutes, or until the cheese has melted. Garnish with some of the avocados and dollops of sour cream, and serve.

Molasses-Glazed Chicken Wings

Yield: 20 wings

These mahogany-brown wings are addictive! They're great for parties or to keep in the fridge for late-night, post-Cowboy Cocktail snacks.

> 20 chicken wings, about 2 to 3 pounds
> $^1/_4$ cup vegetable oil
> 1 cup Molasses Rub

Molasses Rub

> 1 cup packed brown sugar
> 2 tablespoons molasses
> 2 teaspoons paprika
> 2 teaspoons dried thyme
> 1 teaspoon garlic powder
> $1^1/_2$ teaspoons kosher salt
> $1^1/_2$ teaspoons freshly ground black pepper

Preheat the oven to 375°F. In a food processor or blender, combine the ingredients for the rub and process until the mixture is well blended.

In a large bowl, toss the chicken wings and oil together until the wings are completely coated. Add the molasses rub and toss again until all the wings are coated. Place the seasoned wings in a large roasting pan and bake for 35 to 40 minutes, or until wings are done through with no trace of pink remaining at the bone.

molasses-glazed chicken

wings

Sliders

Yield: 24 mini-burgers

Sliders are mini-burgers that are served on biscuits instead of hamburger buns. They may be small, but they pack a lot of flavor!

The Burgers

Follow the recipe for CF Burgers on page 105, making the burgers $^1/_4$ of the size described in the recipe.

The Buns

3 packages refrigerated biscuit dough
Condiments: Red Chile Mayo (page 120), Fruit Mustard (page 120), or Marinated Tomatoes (page 115), or your favorite bottled ketchups, relishes, and mustards.

Bake the biscuits according to the package instructions. When they are done, set aside to cool for a few minutes (so they don't crumble) before slicing in half horizontally. Top with a cooked mini-burger and your condiments of choice.

COWBOY VOCABULARY:

Names for the camp cook: dough wrangler, cookie, sourdough, bean-master, hasher, grub-slinger, dough-roller.

SPICY CABBAGE

Yield: 4 cups

This is a sharp, refreshing variation on the traditional shredded cabbage used in Mexican cooking as a condiment or side salad. The rice vinegar is important, because it is sweet and contrasts nicely with the bite of the jalapeño. For maximum crunch value, make this the day you plan to serve it.

> 4 cups finely shredded white or red cabbage (or 2 cups of each)
> 1/2 red onion, sliced paper thin
> 1 jalapeño pepper, stemmed, seeded, and diced
> 2 tablespoons olive oil
> 1 tablespoon seasoned rice vinegar

In a large glass or stainless steel bowl, combine all the ingredients and toss thoroughly to combine.

MARINATED TOMATOES

Yield: 10 to 15 slices

These are great for the grazing crowd. Don't try to do this in the middle of winter—you want to use the best tomatoes you can find or grow.

> 2 or 3 large, ripe beefsteak tomatoes
> 1/2 cup balsamic vinegar
> 2 tablespoons minced garlic
> 2 tablespoons minced fresh thyme
> 1/2 teaspoon kosher salt, or to taste
> 3/4 cup vegetable oil

Core the tomatoes, cut them into fairly thick slices, and set aside. In a large stainless steel or glass bowl, whisk together the vinegar, garlic, thyme, and salt. Slowly add the vegetable oil in a thin stream, whisking constantly until it is completely incorporated. Add the tomato slices, turning them gently to be sure they are completely coated with marinade, but be careful not to break them up. Cover tightly with plastic wrap, and refrigerate for at least 2 hours before serving. Tomatoes will keep in the refrigerator for up to 2 days.

sides...

SPICY PECANS

Yield: 4 cups

At Reata, we serve these pecans on a salad with goat cheese and tomatoes, but Grady's friend Jaime Adams swears he can eat two pounds by themselves on any given night! Try serving them at the bar with some Cowboy Cocktails and watch them disappear.

- **4 cups (about 1 pound) shelled pecan halves**
- **6 tablespoons unsalted butter, melted**
- **4 teaspoons chile powder**
- **$^1/_2$ cup packed brown sugar**

Preheat the oven to 350°F. In a large bowl, toss the pecans in the melted butter until they are completely coated. Sprinkle the chile powder over the nuts and toss to coat them completely. Add the sugar and toss with your hands to keep the sugar from forming lumps. Spread the mixture out onto a lightly oiled baking sheet, scraping the residue from the bowl on top of the nuts. Bake for 20 minutes, or until the nuts begin to brown and the butter begins to spread. At this point, the coating won't be crunchy, but as the nuts cool, the coating will harden. The nuts can be stored in an airtight container for up to 2 weeks.

MESCAL PRALINES

Yield: 2 dozen pralines

These are pralines for adults! The mescal is subtle, but definitely there.

- **$1^1/_2$ cups heavy cream**
- **$1^1/_2$ cups white granulated sugar**
- **$1^1/_2$ cups brown sugar**
- **$^1/_2$ cup mescal**
- **2 tablespoons unsalted butter**
- **2 cups shelled pecans**

Line two large baking sheets with kitchen parchment. In a medium saucepan over low heat, combine the cream, white and brown sugars, and the mescal. Stir the mixture until the sugars have completely dissolved. Cover the pan, increase the heat to medium-high, and cook for about 3 minutes, or until the steam has washed down any crystals from the sides of the pan. Uncover, lower heat, and cook slowly, *without stirring*, until the mixture reaches 260°F on a candy thermometer. Remove from the heat and let cool for 5 minutes.

Stir in the butter, and let the mixture cool to 110°F. Beat with a whisk until the mixture begins to lose its gloss and thicken, then quickly stir in the pecans. Drop the candy mixture in 3-inch circles onto the prepared pans and set aside to cool. When the candies have hardened, wrap in foil and place in an airtight container. Store at room temperature for up to 1 week.

PICO DE GALLO

Yield: 2 cups

This basic salsa goes with just about anything—beef, pork, chicken, or even fish. It's best made the day you plan to serve it.

> 5 jalapeño peppers, stemmed, seeded, and diced
> 1 cup diced tomatoes
> $^3/_4$ cup diced red onions
> $^1/_2$ cup diced jicama
> $^1/_2$ cup chopped fresh cilantro
> Juice of 2 limes
> $^3/_4$ teaspoon kosher salt, or to taste

In a mixing bowl, thoroughly combine all the ingredients. Cover and refrigerate for 1 or 2 hours before serving. This salsa will keep for 24 hours in the refrigerator.

AVOCADO SOUR CREAM

Yield: 4 cups

Serve this emerald-green, rich, and luscious spread with raw vegetable sticks, crackers, or tortilla chips. For an eye-popping variation, layer with your favorite bottled or fresh salsa and shredded Cheddar and Jack cheese in a straight-sided glass bowl. The layers are mouth-watering to look at and dig into.

> 2 ripe avocados, seeded and peeled
> $1^1/_2$ cups sour cream
> $^1/_2$ cup heavy whipping cream
> 1 teaspoon kosher salt, or to taste
> $^1/_2$ teaspoon Tabasco, or to taste
> 2 tablespoons snipped chives (optional)

Combine the avocados, sour cream, and heavy cream in a food processor or blender and process until smooth. Add the salt, Tabasco, and chives. Taste for seasoning. Store in an airtight container in the refrigerator until ready to serve (serve within 8 hours).

guacamole

de ojinaga

GUACAMOLE DE OJINAGA

Yield: 4 cups

At the Reata restaurant in Alpine we do our shopping in Ojinaga, Mexico—just across the border from Presidio. One of Grady's favorite sauces is "Maggi," which is sort of like a Mexican soy sauce. When in Ojinaga, we always buy some to bring home, but you can find it in any market with Latin American groceries.

2 to 3 red bell peppers, for garnish
4 ripe avocados, seeded and peeled
1 ripe tomato, seeded and diced
$^1/_2$ red onion, finely diced
3 jalapeño peppers, stemmed, seeded, and finely diced
$^1/_2$ cup cilantro leaves, finely chopped
2 tablespoons Maggi or soy sauce
Juice of 2 fresh limes
Kosher salt to taste (remember the Maggi is salty, so go easy)

Preheat broiler. Place peppers in a roasting pan and roast in broiler until charred all over. Transfer to a bowl and cover tightly with plastic wrap. Let steam for 15 minutes. Peel peppers (skin will lift away easily). Stem and remove seeds. Cut peppers into strips and set aside.

In a large mixing bowl, mash the avocados by hand with a fork. Add the remaining ingredients and combine thoroughly. Refrigerate in an airtight container for 1 hour before serving to let the flavor develop. Garnish with the roasted peppers and serve with fresh tortilla or taco chips, or spread on bread with some fresh field greens for a healthy sandwich.

Note: This guacamole should not be puréed. It should be satisfyingly chunky.

FRUIT MUSTARD

Yield: 2 cups

Use this festive mustard to give hamburgers and hot dogs a serious wake-up call at your next trail-ride picnic or tail-gate party. For a fabulous salad dressing, make this in the food processor and add 1 cup of your favorite vinegar and 3 cups combined olive and vegetable oil.

- **1 cup Dijon mustard**
- **2 tablespoons honey**
- **$^1/_4$ cup apricot preserves**
- **2 jalapeño peppers, stemmed, seeded, and finely diced**
- **$^1/_2$ red bell pepper, seeded and finely diced**
- **1 green onion, white and light green part only, finely chopped**
- **2 tablespoons finely chopped fresh cilantro**

Warm a large mixing bowl with hot water, then pour off the water (this will allow the honey to flow more easily). Add all the ingredients and whisk with a fork until thoroughly blended. Keep refrigerated in an airtight container for up to 3 days.

RED CHILE MAYO

Yield: 1 cup

Who says mayonnaise has to be boring—or even white? Try this the next time you're making egg salad sandwiches for a picnic or to put a little "devil" in the deviled eggs at your next party.

- **1 large egg, separated**
- **Juice of 1 lime**
- **$^3/_4$ cup vegetable oil**
- **$^1/_2$ teaspoon salt**
- **1 teaspoon good-quality red chile sauce**

Place the egg yolk and the lime juice in a blender or food processor. While blending on the lowest speed, slowly add the vegetable oil in a thin stream (it is important to add these to the egg slowly so that the mixture will completely emulsify and not separate later). Continue to blend, adding the salt and chile sauce. If the mixture becomes too thick, you can thin it with water—more oil will only make it thicker! Store in an airtight container in the refrigerator for up to 2 days before using.

CILANTRO-PECAN MASH

Yield: 2 cups

A spread by any other name is a mash in Texas, and this nutty, cheesy mash has enough of a zing to liven up any boring cocktail party.

> 1 cup (about $^1/_4$ pound)
>   pecan pieces
> 1 bunch fresh cilantro,
>   coarsely chopped
> $^3/_4$ cup vegetable oil
> $^1/_4$ cup grated Asiago cheese
> 1 tablespoon minced garlic
> $^3/_4$ teaspoon kosher salt, or
>   to taste

Preheat the oven to 350°F. Spread the pecan pieces on a baking sheet and bake for 10 minutes, checking them midway to be sure they don't burn. Let cool for 5 minutes. Place the pecans in a food processor or blender and chop. Add the remaining ingredients and process until a spreadable paste forms. Taste for seasoning. If the spread becomes too thin, add a little more cheese. If it is too thick, add a teaspoon of water at a time until the correct consistency is reached. Serve with crackers.

SUNFLOWER SEED MASH

Yield: 2 cups

Try this tasty, healthy spread on small pieces of toast for a south of the border bruschetta, and see if your guests can figure out what it is.

> 1 cup raw sunflower seeds
> 1 cup vegetable oil
> $^1/_2$ cup chopped fresh spinach
>   (make sure it is well
>   rinsed!)
> $^1/_2$ cup grated Asiago cheese
> 3 jalapeño peppers, stemmed,
>   seeded, and diced
> 2 tablespoons minced garlic
> $^3/_4$ teaspoon kosher salt, or
>   to taste

Preheat oven to 350°F. Spread the sunflower seeds on a baking sheet and sprinkle with 2 tablespoons of the oil. Toast in the oven for 10 minutes, watching carefully that they do not scorch. Let cool for 5 minutes. In a blender or food processor, combine the seeds with the remaining oil and the spinach, cheese, peppers, garlic, and salt. Process until a spreadable paste forms. The mash will keep, covered and refrigerated, for up to 3 days.

SUNDRIED TOMATO MASH

Yield: 2 cups

Don't let the brown color of this versatile spread-mash-dip fool you— it tastes delicious. Use it as a spread on your favorite sandwich or burger, or as a dip for vegetables. One favorite use is as a rub for barbecued chicken. Just slather it on the chicken pieces, throw them on the grill, and presto, great flavor.

> $^1/_2$ **cup dry-packed sundried tomatoes**
> **1 cup spinach, roughly chopped**
> **3 jalapeño peppers, stemmed, seeded, and diced**
> **2 tablespoons minced garlic**
> $^3/_4$ **teaspoon kosher salt**
> **1 cup vegetable oil**

Place the sundried tomatoes in a small bowl of warm water. Set aside for 10 minutes to rehydrate. Squeeze out the excess water.

In a food processor or blender, combine the tomatoes, spinach, peppers, garlic, salt, and oil. Process, scraping down the bowl as necessary, until a spreadable paste is formed. Refrigerate, tightly covered, for up to 3 days and serve on crackers, toast triangles, or tortilla chips.

REATA GRILL BLEND

Yield: 1 cup

Some chefs call it their "essence," but Grady is a little more down to earth about his seasoning mixture. Make up a batch of this flavorful stuff and you'll be using it on everything from steaks destined for the grill to baked potatoes to a scoop of cottage cheese for breakfast. It's also super for quick and simple cooking in the great out-of-doors—take some on your next camping trip.

> **4 tablespoons kosher salt**
> **3 tablespoons Pasilla or other strong chile powder**
> **2 tablespoons dried granulated garlic**
> **2 tablespoons sugar**
> **2 tablespoons ground cumin**
> **2 tablespoons coarsely ground black pepper**
> **1 tablespoon ground thyme**

In a small bowl, combine all the ingredients, blending well to evenly distribute all the spices. Be sure to break up any chunks that form. Store the blend in an airtight container. Shake or stir it again before each use. Keeps for up to 3 months.

CHIPOTLE BBQ SAUCE

Yield: 4 cups

This recipe was kept close to Grady's heart for a long, long time—but he eventually let it be published in A Cowboy in the Kitchen. *Here it is again, because it's one of the all-time great BBQ sauces and we use it in just about all our cooking (except desserts, so far).*

    1 tablespoon oil
    2 cups diced yellow onion
    7 cloves garlic, minced
    1 cup ketchup
    1 cup puréed Chipotles Chiles en Adobo (see Note)
    $^1/_2$ cup Worcestershire sauce
    $^1/_2$ cup strong coffee
    $^1/_3$ cup packed brown sugar
    $^1/_4$ cup cider vinegar
    $^1/_4$ cup freshly squeezed lemon juice
    1$^1/_2$ tablespoons Dijon mustard
    2 teaspoons Kosher salt

Heat the oil in a large, heavy saucepan over medium heat. Add the onion and garlic and sauté until they begin to wilt. Add the ketchup and chile paste and sauté for 4 minutes. Add all of the remaining ingredients, stir, and let the mixture simmer, stirring occasionally, for 30 to 40 minutes. As the sauce thickens, stir more often so it does not scorch. Remove the sauce from the heat and let cool. Place the sauce in a blender and purée. Store in an airtight container in the refrigerator for up to 4 days.

Note: Canned Chipotle Chiles en Adobo are available in many Latin American and other well-stocked markets. Scoop all the contents of the can, including all the sauce, into a blender or food processor and purée until smooth.

ONION MARMALADE

Yield: 5 cups

Sweet, luscious, and tangy all at the same time, this onion "jam" goes particularly well with the flavor of goat cheese. We like to mix them half and half and stuff the result under the skin of a quail, or you could try it with chicken. The same mixture makes a superb spread for a hearty (though, actually, it's vegetarian) portobello mushroom sandwich.

> 2 large red onions (about 1^1/$_2$ pounds)
> 2 large yellow onions (about 1^1/$_2$ pounds)
> 4 bunches scallions, green parts only
> 3 tablespoons olive oil
> 1^1/$_2$ cups balsamic vinegar
> ^{1}/$_4$ cup brown sugar
> Kosher salt to taste
> Freshly ground pepper to taste

Peel the onions and trim the root ends. Stand each onion on its root end and slice through the center, top to bottom. Continue thinly slicing each half in this fashion to produce thin, semicircular julienne slices. Thinly slice the green part of the scallion.

Heat the olive oil in a large skillet over medium heat. Add the onions and the scallions and toss to coat with oil. Sauté until the onions begin to soften, then cover the pan and cook until they are wilted. Remove the lid, increase the heat, and add the vinegar. Cook until the vinegar reduces by one half, stirring occasionally. Add the sugar, salt, and pepper and stir well. Taste the mixture; it should be sweet and sour. Onions have different amounts of natural sugar at different times of the year, so you may need to adjust the amount of sugar to taste. Reduce the heat to low and continue cooking the mixture until the liquid is almost absorbed and the marmalade is thick, about 10 minutes. Remove from the heat and serve. Store any extra in a jar in the refrigerator for up to 1 week.

The Cowboy Cocktails Movie Thee-ater

The Alamo, 1960 *** ¹/₂
A John Wayne-fest

El Dorado, 1967 **** ¹/₂
John Wayne, Robert Mitchum

Giant, 1956 *** ¹/₂
Edna Ferber's compelling Texas epic; Rock Hudson, Elizabeth Taylor, James Dean. Read the book, too, for the full experience.

High Noon, 1952 *****
Gary Cooper classic

Lonesome Dove, 1989 *****
Robert Duvall and Tommy Lee Jones. 'Nuff said.

The Magnificent Seven, 1960 ****
Talk about star-studded; Yul Bryner, Steve McQueen, James Coburn, Eli Wallach, Charles Bronson

Rancho Deluxe, 1975 ***
Western comedy; Jeff Bridges, Sam Waterston, with a soundtrack and cameo by Jimmy Buffett

The Cowboy Cocktails Reading Room

Cimarron Rose: A Novel
by James Lee Burke
Hyperion, 1998

Cowboys Are My Weakness
by Pam Houston
Washington Square Press, 1993

Fixin' to Be Texan
by Helen Bryant
Republic of Texas Press, 1998

Giant
by Edna Ferber
Buccaneer Books, 1952

God Bless John Wayne
by Kinky Friedman
Bantam Books, 1996

Lonesome Dove
by Larry McMurtry
Pocket Books, 1991

Texas
by James A. Michener
Fawcett Books, 1994

9

BASIC RECIPES AND GARNISHES

*he following garnishes and basic preparations are called for in various drink recipes in the book.

KAHLUA CREAM

Yield: 1 quart

This luscious topping is superb on any coffee drink, whether it contains Kahlua, Tia Maria, or just plain coffee. Use the Crème de Naranja variation on coffee and mocha drinks for a shot of that superb orange-chocolate-coffee magic.

1 quart heavy cream
4 tablespoons powdered sugar
2 $^1/_2$ ounces Kahlua

Pour the heavy cream into the bowl of an electric mixer with the whip attachment in place. Whip the cream on high speed until soft peaks form, 2 to 3 minutes. Slowly add the powered sugar and Kahlua and continue to whip for another $1^1/_2$ to 2 minutes, until very stiff (do not whip so long that the cream turns to butter). Remove the whipped cream from the bowl and refrigerate.

VARIATION: to make Crème de Naranja, substitute Grand Marnier, Curaçao, or good Triple Sec for the Kahlua.

REATA SWEET 'N' SOUR MIX

Yield: 4 cups

Every good bartender has their own sweet-and-sour mix that they swear by, and the Reata bartenders are no different. You may want to adjust the sweet/sour balance to reflect your own personal taste—and then it will become your *special sweet-and-sour mix!*

> 3 cups sugar
> 4 cups water
> 2 cinnamon sticks
> 1¹/₂ cups freshly squeezed lime juice

In a large saucepan, combine the sugar, water, and cinnamon and stir until the sugar has dissolved. Bring the mixture to a boil over medium-high heat. Reduce the heat so the mixture simmers and add the lime juice. Cook gently for 4 or 5 minutes more, then remove from heat and let cool. When cool, remove the cinnamon sticks (these can be rinsed, dried, and reused) and pour into a covered container. Refrigerate for up to 1 week.

REATA'S FAMOUS BLOODY MARY MIX

Yield: 5 cups

Just like a good sweet-and-sour mix, all good bartenders must have a great Bloody Mary mix in their repertoire to be taken seriously. We've generously shared ours (developed over many months of careful testing) with you here.

> 1 quart good-quality tomato juice
> 6 ounces Worcestershire sauce
> 1 ounce freshly squeezed lemon juice
> 2 tablespoons Tabasco sauce
> 1 tablespoon red pepper flakes
> 1 tablespoon cracked black pepper
> 1 teaspoon dried dill, or two teaspoons chopped fresh dill
> ¹/₄ cup grated fresh horse-radish

In a blender, combine all the ingredients and blend for 1 minute. Use as needed. The mix will last for up to 2 days, covered and refrigerated.

SIMPLE SYRUP

Yield: 2 cups

This versatile syrup is on every serious home bar and all commercial bars. The reason for simple syrup is that many, many drinks contain sugar to balance the strong (the alcohol) and the sour (usually lime or some other citrus) flavors. Since most drinks are cold, and sugar doesn't melt very efficiently in cold water, we have simple syrup (the sugar has already been melted). If a recipe calls for 1 teaspoon of sugar, just use 1 teaspoon of simple syrup. (By the way, this stuff is superb for sweetening iced tea, the official non-alcoholic drink of Texas.)

> 2 cups granulated sugar
> 2 cups water

In a small saucepan over low heat, combine the sugar and water. Stir until the sugar has dissolved and the mixture turns clear. Increase the heat and bring the mixture to a boil. Remove from the heat and let cool. Store in a clean, sealable glass container. The syrup will keep indefinitely at room temperature.

CINNAMON STARS

Yield: 12 to 16 stars

Float these fun little garnishes on top of the Drugstore Cowboy Shake (page 11) or any other drink where the cinnamon will happily match with the other flavors.

> 4 (8-inch) flour tortillas
> 2 tablespoons ground cinnamon
> 2 tablespoons granulated sugar
> Vegetable oil for frying

Using a star cookie cutter, cut 3 or 4 stars out of each tortilla. In a small bowl, combine the sugar and the cinnamon and set aside. In a large skillet over high heat, heat $1/2$ inch of vegetable oil to 350° F. Gently place a few stars in the oil and fry for 2 or 3 minutes, turning once, until golden brown. Be careful not to let the stars stick to the bottom of the pan. Remove the stars from the oil and pat dry with a paper towel. While the stars are still hot, dust with the cinnamon and sugar mixture, then set aside. Continue with the remaining stars. Keep the stars uncovered (this will keep them from getting soggy) at room temperature for 3 or 4 days.

CANDIED LIMES

Yield: 1 cup

If piloncello (a popular Mexican sugar that comes in little cone shapes) is unavailable in your area, substitute equal parts brown sugar and ground cinnamon. These make a lovely garnish for drinks like Texas Lemonade and can be added to any concoction that contains lime juice and a sweet element.

> **2 cups granulated sugar**
> **1¹/₂ cup water**
> **3 limes, thinly sliced (ends discarded)**
> **2 tablespoons grated piloncello**

In a large, heavy saucepan over high heat, combine the sugar and water. Bring the mixture to a boil, then reduce the heat so the mixture is just simmering. Add the lime slices and cook gently for 25 to 30 minutes, until softened but with plenty of liquid remaining. Remove the pan from the heat and let cool for 15 minutes. With a slotted spoon, transfer the lime slices to a baking sheet or large plate. Dust each lime slice with the piloncello and let cool for 20 to 30 minutes. Use immediately or keep covered, at room temperature, for 4 or 5 days.

PICKLED JALAPEÑO PEPPERS

Yield: 4 peppers

An acquired taste. Don't drop these into cocktails with wild abandon— judge the moment carefully.

> **¹/₂ cup white vinegar**
> **¹/₂ cup pineapple juice**
> **2 tablespoons brown sugar**
> **4 firm, fresh jalapeño peppers, washed**

In a small saucepan over low heat, combine the vinegar, pineapple juice, and sugar. Stir until the sugar has dissolved. Add the peppers, increase the heat, and bring the mixture to a boil. Simmer for 5 minutes, then remove from the heat and let cool completely. If desired, transfer the peppers to a sterilized jar, cover it tightly, and keep refrigerated for up to 2 weeks. This recipe can be doubled or even tripled.

Photo Credits

COVER *Top:* By Russell Lee, 1903, Courtesy the Library of Congress, American Memory Collection *Bottom:* Copyright © 1985 by Jose Azel, used by permission of Aurora, Picture Network International Ltd. *Back:* By Richard E. Ahlborn, American Folklife Center, Library of Congress

PAGE iii By Russell Lee, 1903, Courtesy the Library of Congress, American Memory Collection

PAGE iv By Russell Lee, 1903, Courtesy the Library of Congress, American Memory Collection

PAGE v Courtesy Glenbow Archives, Calgary, Canada (NB (H)-16-452)

PAGE vi By Russell Lee, 1903, Courtesy the Library of Congress, American Memory Collection

PAGE 5 By Russell Lee, 1903, Courtesy the Library of Congress, American Memory Collection

PAGE 8 *Top:* Copyright © 1999 by Kathleen Jo Ryan from *Deep in the Heart of Texas: Texas Ranchers in Their Own Words* *Bottom:* Copyright © 1998 by Rick Najdzion, Cowboy Up Photos

PAGE 17 By Richard E. Ahlborn, American Folklife Center, Library of Congress

PAGE 20 *Top:* Copyright © 1996 by Randy Wells, used by permission of AllStock, Picture Network International Ltd. *Bottom:* Copyright © 1991 by Charles Pefley, used by permission of Stock, Boston, Inc., Picture Network International Ltd.

PAGE 23 Copyright © 1995, 1996 by Del Maguey Ltd., used with permission.

PAGE 36 *Top:* Copyright © 1990 by Gary E. Holscher, used by permission of AllStock, Picture Network International Ltd. *Bottom:* Copyright © 1992 by C. Bruce Forster, used by permission of AllStock, Picture Network International Ltd.

PAGE 48 *Top:* Corbis Images, Royalty Free *Bottom:* Corbis Images, Royalty Free

PAGE 60 *Top:* Corbis Images, Royalty Free *Bottom:* Copyright © 1999 by Joe Sohm/Chromosohm, used by permission of Stock Connection, Picture Network International Ltd.

PAGE 74 *Top:* Copyright © 1990 by Jeffry Scott, used by permission of Impact Visuals, Picture Network International Ltd. *Bottom:* By Kent Barker, used by permission of The Image Bank, Inc., Picture Network International Ltd.

PAGE 84 *Top:* Copyright © 1985 by Jose Azel, used by permission of Aurora, Picture Network International Ltd. *Bottom:* Corbis Images, Royalty Free

PAGE 94 *Top:* Copyright © 1998 by Charles Gullung, used by permission of Nonstock, Inc., Picture Network International Ltd. *Bottom:* Copyright © 1989 by Caroline Wood, used by permission of AllStock, Picture Network International Ltd.

PAGE 126 *Top:* Copyright © 1993 by Joanna Pinneo, used by permission of Aurora, Picture Network International Ltd. *Bottom:* Corbis Images, Royalty Free

⭐ Index

The Rising Star from the Lone Star State

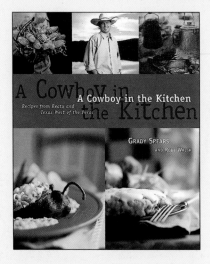

F ROM TEXAS COMES HOT NEW TALENT GRADY SPEARS, who went from riding and roping on the open range to creating his own vision of cowboy cuisine at the Reata restaurants in Alpine and Fort Worth, Texas (and soon in Beverly Hills, California).

Grady's food is authentic, down-home cowboy cooking, but with a decidedly uptown twist.

★ ★ ★ ★ ★ ★ ★ ★ ★ ★ ★ ★ ★ ★